THE FACE
and the
GLORY

LESSONS ON THE INVISIBLE AND VISIBLE GOD AND HIS GLORY

GREG HARRIS

© 2019 Gregory H. Harris
The Face and the Glory
Lessons on the Invisible and Visible God
And His Glory

All rights reserved. No portion of this book may be reproduced in any form without the written permission of the publisher except for brief excerpts quoted in critical reviews.

Kress Biblical Resources
The Woodlands, Texas
www.kressbiblical.com

ISBN: 978-1-934952-45-0

Scripture taken from the NEW AMERICAN STANDARD BIBLE®, Copyright © 1960,1962,1963,1968,1971,1972,1973,1975,1977 by The Lockman Foundation. Used by permission.

For Rob Thurman

But He said, "You cannot see My face, for no man can see Me and live."

—*Exodus 33:20*

Since then no prophet has risen in Israel like Moses, whom the L<small>ORD</small> *knew face to face.*

—*Deuteronomy 34:10*

"In the year of King Uzziah's death, I saw the Lord sitting on a throne, lofty and exalted, with the train of His robe filling the temple."

Then I said, "Woe is me, for I am ruined! Because I am a man of unclean lips, and I live among a people of unclean lips;

For my eyes have seen the King, the L<small>ORD</small> *of hosts."*

—*Isaiah 6:1, 5*

[God] who alone possesses immortality and dwells in unapproachable light, whom no man has seen or can see.

—*1 Timothy 6:16*

No one has seen God at any time; the only begotten God who is in the bosom of the Father, He has explained Him.

—*John 1:18*

ACKNOWLEDGMENTS

Dr. Greg Harris' personal editor: Rebecca R. Howard.

Dr. Greg Harris' personal website: www.glorybooks.org.

"The Master's Seminary consulting class," Spring 2019 (We didn't actually have a TMS consulting class this time around, but I went ahead and used the term anyway): Bob and Julie Fanciullacci, Becky Howard, Nancy Anderson—and those untimely born and grafted in: Jim Rouse, Rob Thurman, Aaron Filburn, and Faly Ravoahangy.

Special thanks to Marty Wolf, for his godly input and for his superb knowledge on Jewish matters past, present, and future.

FOREWORD AND EXPLANATION OF *THE FACE AND THE GLORY*

Almost ten years ago from the writing of the foreword of this book, I began studying and writing about what critics claim to be brazen, unsolvable errors in Scripture, namely that the Bible has verses—sometime even within one chapter—that God cannot be seen and that God can be seen. This intrigued me, as it has intrigued Bible readers and scholars throughout the centuries.

Through a series of unexpected expected developments at work and through multiple surgeries, I had completed only about half of my study when I had to put the material aside for almost ten years. Then—as so often is the case with God—I was unexpectedly encouraged to continue working on it, and now I have finished the material. The biggest problem in writing this new work was that in the meantime I had written in much detail about certain parts of this book in other Glory Books, and they were already published, especially *The Darkness and the Glory*, *The Stone and the Glory*, and *The Stone and the Glory of Israel*. Also, I wrote *The Bible Expositor's Handbook—Digital Old Testament* edition and *The Bible Expositor's Handbook—Digital New Testament* edition. A print version of the combined Handbooks is due out in 2019 or 2020. A volume of biblical teaching is found in these books. Anyone who is interested in any of these can Google the titles to find out how to get the books. All royalties are signed over to

The Master's Academies International for them to use as they see fit. For those who are not familiar with this ministry, we can just use the shortened form for "Foreign Missions."

After the passing of so many years, when I unexpectedly started studying and completing *The Face the Glory*, my biggest fear was that this new book would be somewhat a recapitulation of things already written. What I found was this: (1) there is some overflow of topics in *The Face and the Glory*, but not nearly as much as I thought, (2) when I encountered something that I had already covered in detail, I have made a reference in this book so that someone who wants to make a deeper study of a particular topic can find further information, and finally (3) God took me down different paths so that this new Glory Book contains much new teaching that is not found in my collective writings elsewhere, and this stands alone as its own book. Ironically, this fifth Glory Book may be a good place to start for those who have not read any of the others. I purposely wrote to keep it from having too many pages and can be read in a relatively short time.

As we go through some very important biblical trails about the God who can and cannot be seen, we will see that this new study will increase our understanding of this very important topic, and we will love God more deeply as together we study *The Face and the Glory*, the visible and invisible God—and His glory.

Greg Harris
The Master's Seminary
February 2019

CONTENTS

Acknowledgments vii

Foreword and Explanation of *The Face and the Glory* ix

CHAPTER ONE
    The Enigma 1

CHAPTER TWO
    The Face 11

CHAPTER THREE
    The Peace 29

CHAPTER FOUR
    The Name 49

CHAPTER FIVE
    The Son 63

CHAPTER SIX
    The Companion 87

CHAPTER SEVEN
    The Hiding 99

CHAPTER EIGHT
    The Consideration 123

CHAPTER NINE
    The Eyes 153

CHAPTER TEN
    The Glory 169

CHAPTER ONE

THE ENIGMA

The word "enigma" has various translations such as "a hard mystery; a perplexing riddle; a confusing puzzle." Everyday life is full of enigmas. The wisest unsaved person on the face of the earth cannot fully understand enough to resolve every enigma: to solve every problem; to answer accurately and adequately every riddle; to rid the world of its many puzzling perplexities. The simple truth is only God qualifies in this regard.

So even for those who are saved, it is indeed comforting that "The secret things belong to the Lord our God, but the things revealed belong to us and to our sons forever, that we may observe all the words of this law" (Deut. 29:29). In contrast between the depth of what God knows versus the utterly miniscule degree of what collective fallen humanity knows, God declares, "For My thoughts are not your thoughts, nor are your ways My ways," declares the Lord. "For as the heavens are higher than the earth, so are My ways higher than your ways and My thoughts than your thoughts" (Isa. 55:8–9).

As many of us can testify, before our salvation we continuously used to "walk in darkness" (Isa. 9:2; Eph. 5:7–10), not just in the spiritual darkness of sin (Eph. 2:1–3), but also in utter confusion by life's enigmas because no true hope can be found outside of God and His Word. For example, in our life or in the life of someone we love, a tragedy, such as an unexpected death, may drive us to find answers to the enigma of why "bad things happen to good people."

The entire book of Ecclesiastes springs from the vantage point of "The Preacher," most likely King Solomon, who once walked closely with the LORD, but then stopped walking closely with God because of the king's horrendous sinfulness (1 Kings 11:1–11). The Preacher wrote about the multiple enigmas of life, beginning and concluding his book with this overall assessment of life: "Vanity [uselessness] of vanities, all is vanities" (Eccl. 1:2; 12:8). So this wisest of the wise men with unmatched earthly wisdom granted him by God, never solved any of the enigmas that he observed except by ultimately concluding, "Remember also your Creator in the days of your youth, before the evil days come and the years draw near when you will say, 'I have no delight in them'" (Eccl. 12:1).

Even for those who are saved and who are walking with the Lord, God never promises full disclosure during our limited stay on earth (1 Pet. 1:17). In fact, He requires just the opposite from us. In Romans 1:17 Paul quoted Habakkuk 2:4 stating, "But the righteous man shall live by faith." This statement is important and is often misused: the righteous *shall live* by faith. Not only is the appropriate faith in the finished work of Jesus necessary for anyone's justification, but those who are redeemed must live their entire life by faith. Read Habakkuk 3 where the godly prophet did not understand what God was doing by allowing the wicked Babylonians to murder, pillage, and destroy God's city and God's holy Temple, and yet he ended his prophecy with this wonderful statement of faith in God despite not understanding completely what He was about to do: "Though the fig tree should not blossom, and there be no fruit on the vines, though the yield of the olive should fail, and the fields produce no food, though the flock should be cut off from the fold, and there be no cattle in the stalls, yet I will exult in the LORD, I will rejoice in the God of my salvation" (Hab. 3:17–18). A couple of other verses describing the same thing are First Peter 1:13: "Therefore, gird your minds for action, keep sober in spirit, fix your hope completely on the grace to be brought to you at the revelation of Jesus Christ" coupled with this explanation from First Corinthians 13:12, "For now we see in a mirror dimly, but then face to face; now I know in part, but then I will know fully just as I also have been fully known."

Such faith can be accomplished only by feeding continually on God's Word, by having the washing of the Word (Eph. 5:26), by the transforming and renewing of the mind (Rom. 12:1–2), and by growing in grace and knowledge of the Lord Jesus Christ (2 Pet 3:18). As we study the Bible, we learn that it is impossible for God to lie (Heb. 6:18), and Jesus declared, just hours before His arrest that God's Word is truth (John 17:17). In fact, the psalmist states, in the longest chapter in the Bible, the total expansiveness of God's Word: "The sum of Your word is truth, and every one of Your righteous ordinances is everlasting" (Ps. 119:160).

We do fine reading such verses (for the most part) until we hit a biblical enigma: a deep mystery, a hard riddle, a perplexing puzzle. Among those who read His Word, the one enigma in the Bible that generates perhaps the most debate centers on whether or not God can ever be seen.

That God can never be seen by anyone is clearly evident from the verses cited in the Scripture page at the beginning of this book. When Moses pleaded with God about seeing His glory, God responded by explaining and restricting, "You cannot see My face, for no man can see me and live" (Ex. 33:20). In the beautiful closing section of First Timothy, Paul wrote in reference to God that He "alone possesses immortality and dwells in unapproachable light, whom no man has seen or can see" (1 Tim. 6:16). In First John 4:12 John wrote, "No one has beheld God at any time." In the prologue to his Gospel, John further stated the same restriction but also offered a little hope, having written in John 1:18: "No one has seen God at any time; the only begotten God who is in the bosom of the Father, He has explained Him." Part of the explanation about God that Jesus gave occurs in John 4:24: "God is spirit," which, unless He chooses to manifest through some visible form, would never be visible to anyone. Anyone who reads these verses and accepts God's Word for truly being His Word will have no problem understanding that the Bible clearly teaches that no one ever has seen or ever can see God.

And then we repeatedly encounter this biblical enigma: more verses exist that show that God *can* be seen than those that show that He *cannot* be seen.

Just a sampling of the verses proves this. In Genesis 16:7–14, Abram's slave Hagar had been banished from the camp because she had given birth to a son, and that resulted in Sarai's extreme jealously (Gen. 16:1–6). In a mercy-laden episode where the Angel of the LORD shows Himself for the first time in Scripture, He did so by appearing to the outcast Hagar, comforted and provided for her, and then instructed her to submit and return to Abram's camp, promising her that a great people will come forth from her (Gen. 16:7–12). Most of the Arab peoples trace their heritage back to this chapter. Hagar summarized her utter surprise not only that this account happened, but also that she had lived through it: "Then she called the name of the LORD who spoke to her, 'You are a God who sees'; for she said, 'Have I even remained alive here after seeing Him?'" As often has been the case with such appearances of God, people fully understood that God had indeed appeared to them, although often not understanding why He would do so, but also realizing that they should have died from having seen Him.

The LORD appeared to Abraham in Genesis 18:1–2, accompanied by two of His angels, each of them taking the form of a man, and together they even ate a communal meal (Gen 18:8). The chapter concludes, "And as soon as He [the LORD] had finished speaking to Abraham, the LORD departed, and Abraham returned to his place." The two angels whom God had brought with Him

(Gen. 19:1) proceeded to destroy Sodom and Gomorrah, but first they rescued Lot and his family (Gen. 19:2–16).

A rather long and surprising encounter with God occurs in Genesis 33:24–29:

> Then Jacob was left alone, and a man wrestled with him until daybreak. When he saw that he had not prevailed against him, he touched the socket of his thigh; so the socket of Jacob's thigh was dislocated while he wrestled with him. Then he said, "Let me go, for the dawn is breaking." But he said, "I will not let you go unless you bless me."
>
> So he said to him, "What is your name?" And he said, "Jacob." He said, "Your name shall no longer be Jacob, but Israel; for you have striven with God and with men and have prevailed."
>
> Then Jacob asked him and said, "Please tell me your name." But he said, "Why is it that you ask my name?" And he blessed him there.

Jacob responded as many others would have: "So Jacob named the place Peniel [Hebrew, "The Face of God"] for he said, "I have seen God face to face, yet my life has been preserved" (Gen. 32:30). Although not understanding exactly why he had been granted such an audience, Jacob knew (1) he had looked into the face of God, and (2) in his utter sinfulness, he should have been consumed by God's mere presence, and yet (3) somehow God in His grace permitted him to live.

By the way, just to make sure that people did not try to reduce what transpired in Jacob's encounter in Genesis 32 or to misinterpret it, God offered an additional explanation by means of His prophet hundreds of years later that it was indeed God whom Jacob saw:

> In the womb he took his brother by the heel, and in his maturity he contended with God. Yes, he wrestled with the angel and prevailed; he wept and sought His favor. He found Him at Bethel, and there He spoke with us, even the Lord, the God of hosts; the Lord is His name (Hosea 12:3–5).

I presume that you see the enigma of all this. Which is true: the verses that say that God cannot be seen and has not been seen by any man, or the ones that say that He can be seen and had been seen? How can these two diametrical opposites harmonize into biblical truth?

Let's consider just a few more examples. Some of these we will come back to and consider in more detail later in this book.

Moses gave multiple verses in Scripture in reference to his having seen God. In the burning bush account, Moses was "afraid to look at God" (Ex. 3:6). Exodus 33:11 states, "Thus the Lord used to speak to Moses face to face, just as a man speaks to his friend." In rebuking Moses' brother Aaron and his sister Miriam for their rebellion, God Himself condemned them for their sin by demarking the highly privileged status that Moses enjoyed beyond all others—including them:

> He said, "Hear now My words: If there is a prophet among you, I, the Lord, shall make Myself known to him in a vision. I shall speak with him in a dream.
>
> "Not so, with My servant Moses, he is faithful in all My household; with him I speak mouth to mouth, even openly, and not in dark sayings, *and he beholds the form of the Lord.* Why then were you not afraid to speak against My servant, against Moses?" (Numbers 12:6–8).

Later with the account of the death of Moses, Deuteronomy 34:10 offers this summary explanation of Moses' highly honored status that he enjoyed before God: "Since then no prophet has risen in Israel like Moses, whom the LORD knew face to face." Hebrews 11:27 refers to Moses as "seeing Him who is unseen."

Just a couple of more instances from the Book of Judges should suffice, for now, to show that God indeed did appear to people. In Judges 6 the LORD appeared to Gideon as the Angel of the LORD. As with the others, Gideon eventually knew that it was ultimately God whom he beheld and that he should have died because of this: "When Gideon saw that he was the angel of the LORD, he said, 'Alas O Lord God! For now I have seen the angel of the LORD face to face." Virtually the same response occurred with Samson's parents when they encountered the Angel of the LORD. Samson's father Manoah said to his wife, "We shall surely die, for we have seen God" (Judges 13:22), and as was true for the previous biblical occurrences, they did not die even though they had seen God.

More examples can and will be added in the upcoming chapters, such as Isaiah 6:1: "In the year of King Uzziah's death, *I saw the Lord sitting on a throne,* lofty and exalted, with the train of His robe filling the temple" (Isa. 6:1). Isaiah's response was likewise similar to those responses that we have already seen. Instead of erupting in worshipful adoration, Isaiah exclaimed, "Woe is me for I am ruined! Because I am a man of unclean lips, and I live among a people of unclean lips; *for my eyes have seen the King, the LORD of Hosts*" (Isa. 6:5).

So by means of summary, let us consider the enigma before us. First, from direct quotes in the Bible, it is clearly evident that no one has ever seen or ever can see God. Second, yet the very same Scripture that teaches that God cannot be seen also gives multiple instances where people did see God; in fact, even more references occur for people having seen God than verses that say they cannot see Him.

Which is right?

They both are.

However, while not requiring at this point a Trinity, if the Bible is true—and it most certainly is—even at this point it *requires* at least a Godhead of two members: One who cannot be seen and One who can be seen. Yet this only leads to another enigma. "*The Shema*" of Deuteronomy 6:4 requires: "Hear, O Israel, the LORD is our God; the LORD is one!"

So what do we do with this repeated enigma in the Bible? As stated before, to a large degree it depends on who you are and how you approach the Word of God. For a liberal theologian who holds that there is no such thing as divine inspiration and thus treats the Bible as one would treat any other man-made writing, biblical enigmas only offer overwhelming proof to them that there is nothing unique about the Bible, because it contains multiple falsehoods and contradictions. This is a brazen reprobate theology because it attempts to demean God's Holy Word by placing it on the same level as a good novel or a philosophy book. Ironically, by denying God as the ultimate author, they attempt to pull His Words down on par with their own words. By their conclusion, biblical enigmas are irrelevant because human authors contradicted one another to present a flawed work of literature that we call the Bible. Psalm 18:26 gives part of the reason why God appears so distorted to those who mock Him: "With the pure You show Yourself pure, and with the crooked You show Yourself astute" [literally in the Hebrew text, "twisted"].

For baby Christians, biblical enigmas are "meat not milk" (1 Cor. 3:1–3). They will need a qualified person to instruct them in the deeper teachings of the Word.

As for Word-starved churches, most of them will never study nor hear the Word enough to consider what it says or perhaps even to know that enigmas are there.

But for the lovers of God and His Word, enigmas are *wonderful* because (1) God is not the God of confusion (1 Cor. 14:33); (2) the Bible is His Word, so not only does He know that these enigmas are in Scripture, but He also divinely superintended that the biblical writers made sure that the enigmas were included in His holy Word; (3) and because God Himself (and not, for instance, Moses) placed these enigmas in His Word, these apparent contradictions virtually always—if studied properly—lead to a better understanding of the attributes and activities of the Godhead—and they often result in worshipful praise issuing forth. Finally, (4) since "the testimony of Jesus is the spirit of prophecy" (Rev. 19:10), and all the prophets spoke regarding Him (Luke 24:27, 44–45), we should not be surprised that amazing and worship-evoking truths about Jesus the Messiah emerge—which they do—when we encounter these sublime biblical enigmas face to face.

CHAPTER TWO

THE FACE

When God ratified the eternally important Abrahamic Covenant in Genesis 15:12–21, forever granting to Abraham's lineage the land, seed, and worldwide blessing that God would bring about (Gen. 12:1–3), He also did something that most people fail to see in the text: He established the timeline and general framework for the Book of Exodus. Genesis 15:13–14 reveals, "And God said to Abram, 'Know for certain that your descendants will be strangers in a land that is not theirs, where they will be enslaved and oppressed four hundred years. But I will also judge the nation whom they will serve; and afterward they will come out with many possessions.'" Genesis 15:16 adds another component of God's promise: "Then in the fourth generation they shall return here, for the iniquity of the Amorite is not yet complete." This last verse is vitally important in that two parts of the divine promise must transpire or else God is not true and powerful: not only must He redeem the yet-to-be-enslaved nation (which did not even exist at the time of this promise) out of their physical bondage, He must also bring them back into the very land where He ratified the Abrahamic Covenant. If He failed in either of these two declarations (or in anything else), He is not fully God and His Word does not matter.

Thus, before God performed any of His mighty deeds in Egypt, before He commissioned Moses at the burning bush, a reminder from God's Word as to what He was getting ready to do, and even more so why He was doing it, emerges. Exodus 2:24–25 concludes the chapter by stating, "So God heard their groaning; and God remembered His covenant with Abraham, Isaac, and Jacob. And God saw the sons of Israel, and God took notice of them." This is vastly more than a book about the horrors of slavery and the freedom that God wrought for the Jewish people or for other people groups. Notice how both components of what God had promised in Genesis 15 are found when He addressed Moses in the burning bush encounter: "So I have come down to deliver them from the power of the Egyptians, *and* to bring them up from that land to a good and spacious land, to a land flowing with milk and honey, to the place of the Canaanite and the Hittite and the Amorite and the Perizzite and the Hivite and the Jebusite" (Ex. 3:8). The deliverance out of Egyptian bondage was only the first part of God's promise; He *must* bring them into the Promised Land to fulfill the second part of His divine decree. It is also of utmost importance to understand that God Himself was the ultimate deliverer—not Moses. God would use Moses, but Moses was only a choice vessel who was neither strong enough, pure enough, nor capable enough by himself to fulfill any of the promises that God had made. Fortunately, however, God was and is able to fulfill all that He promised, both then and now.

So God brought the people out of Egypt and to Mount Sinai, fulfilling the first part of His promise: "In the third month after the sons of Israel had gone out of the land of Egypt, on that very day they came into the wilderness of Sinai. When they set out from Rephidim, they came to the wilderness of Sinai, and camped in the wilderness; and there Israel camped in front of the mountain" (Ex. 19:1–2). Of even greater importance is how God viewed the newly freed Jewish people in relation to Himself: "You yourselves have seen what I did to the Egyptians, and how I bore you on eagles' wings, *and brought you to Myself*" (Ex. 19:4). This blessed personal relationship with God Himself was of much greater importance than their physical redemption from Egypt.

Yet in spite of the personal presence of God, the core fact remains: God is holy; the people were sinful. Consequently, God set the parameters for the way in which He was to be approached and for the restrictions to Himself that He had ordained. The nation, having been physically redeemed, needed next to consecrate themselves unto the Lord their God:

> And the LORD said to Moses, "Behold, I shall come to you in a thick cloud, in order that the people may hear when I speak with you, and may also believe in you forever." Then Moses told the words of the people to the LORD.
>
> The LORD also said to Moses, "Go to the people and consecrate them today and tomorrow, and let them wash their garments; and let them be ready for the third day, for on the third day the LORD will come down on Mount Sinai in the sight of all the people.
>
> "And you shall set bounds for the people all around, saying, 'Beware that you do not go up on the mountain or touch the border of it; whoever touches the mountain shall surely be put to death. No hand shall touch him, but he shall surely be stoned or shot through; whether beast or man, he shall not live. When the ram's horn sounds a long blast, they shall come up to the mountain.'"
>
> So Moses went down from the mountain to the people and consecrated the people, and they washed their garments. And he said to the people, "Be ready for the third day; do not go near a woman" (Ex. 19:9–15).

God explained what happened next in Exodus 19:16–17: "So it came about on the third day, when it was morning, that there were thunder and lightning flashes and a thick cloud upon the mountain and a very loud trumpet sound, so that all the people who were in the camp trembled. And Moses brought the people out of the camp to meet God, and they stood at the foot of the mountain." Note again the personal relationship aspect of this event that God desired: "Moses brought the people out of the camp to meet God."

The Bible gives more details elsewhere about the fearful terror that God evoked in the people, as Moses explained in Deuteronomy 5:22–27:

> These words the Lord spoke to all your assembly at the mountain from the midst of the fire, of the cloud and of the thick gloom, with a great voice, and He added no more. He wrote them on two tablets of stone and gave them to me. And when you heard the voice from the midst of the darkness, while the mountain was burning with fire, you came near to me, all the heads of your tribes and your elders.
>
> You said, "Behold, the Lord our God has shown us His glory and His greatness, and we have heard His voice from the midst of the fire; we have seen today that God speaks with man, yet he lives. Now then why should we die? For this great fire will consume us; if we hear the voice of the Lord our God any longer, then we will die. For who is there of all flesh who has heard the voice of the living God speaking from the midst of the fire, as we have, and lived?
>
> "Go near and hear all that the Lord our God says; then speak to us all that the Lord our God speaks to you, and we will hear and do it."

Hebrews 12:18–21 add additional details, especially how Moses trembled at this:

> For you have not come to a mountain that may be touched and to a blazing fire, and to darkness and gloom and whirlwind, and to the blast of a trumpet and the sound of words which sound was such that those who heard begged that no further word should be spoken to them. For they could not bear the command, "If even a beast touches the mountain, it will be stoned." And so terrible was the sight, that Moses said, "I am full of fear and trembling."

So even Moses, in spite of being God's anointed representative, is included in this fearful trembling before the God who had brought them out of bondage.

The Exodus account also describes the effects of God's presence as He descended on Sinai in Exodus 19:18–20:

> Now Mount Sinai was all in smoke because the LORD descended upon it in fire; and its smoke ascended like the smoke of a furnace, and the whole mountain quaked violently. When the sound of the trumpet grew louder and louder, Moses spoke and God answered him with thunder. The LORD came down on Mount Sinai, to the top of the mountain; and the LORD called Moses to the top of the mountain, and Moses went up.

Note the importance of the next verse as it relates to the people who were not being allowed to look at God: "Then the LORD spoke to Moses, 'Go down, warn the people, so that they do not break through to the LORD to gaze, and many of them perish'" (Ex. 19:21)—as we would expect from the previous verses stating that no one can look at God and live.

So by way of summary, God did indeed redeem His people by fulfilling the first part of what He had promised. He did make a special manifestation of His presence on the Holy Mountain. In this passage there is a sense of the very special presence of God, but also there is an obvious divine separation and prohibition about getting too close to Him, because of His holiness, let alone about looking upon Him.

It is within this context and setting that the Mosaic Covenant (often designated in Scripture as "The Law of Moses" or just the "The Law") would be ratified in Exodus 24:1–8. Yet before that took place, God issued the Ten Commandments (Ex. 20) and gave ordinances of the various laws to the people regarding how they were to live with God and one another (Ex. 21:1–23:9). After all, these were newly redeemed slaves who were no longer under the dictates and control of their oppressors; now they had a divine Redeemer who not merely took them out of slavery, but who also watched over them, shepherding them by giving these laws that—if they would obey— He would greatly bless them. This section includes the important institution of observing the Sabbath day (Ex. 23:10–13). Also, from this time onward, God mandated that three times a year the entire nation of Israel was to stop its normal daily routine and commerce and appear before Him, as Exodus 23:14–19 explains:

> "Three times a year you shall celebrate a feast to Me. You shall observe the Feast of Unleavened Bread; for seven days you are to eat unleavened bread, as I commanded you, at the appointed time in the month Abib, for in it you came out of Egypt. And none shall appear before Me empty-handed.
>
> "Also you shall observe the Feast of the Harvest of the first fruits of your labors from what you sow in the field; also the Feast of the Ingathering at the end of the year when you gather in the fruit of your labors from the field.

> "Three times a year all your males shall appear before the Lord God.
>
> "You shall not offer the blood of My sacrifice with leavened bread; nor is the fat of My feast to remain overnight until morning.
>
> "You shall bring the choice first fruits of your soil into the house of the Lord your God. You are not to boil a young goat in the milk of its mother."

These were divine commands—not suggestions—issued by the completely holy God Himself to the newly redeemed Jewish people.

And then in the midst of the account, almost unnoticed and without any fanfare or special demarcation, God promised to send an angel before the people:

> "Behold, I am going to send an angel before you to guard you along the way, and to bring you into the place which I have prepared. Be on your guard before him and obey his voice; do not be rebellious toward him, for he will not pardon your transgression, since My name is in him. But if you will truly obey his voice and do all that I say, then I will be an enemy to your enemies and an adversary to your adversaries.
>
> "For My angel will go before you and bring you in to the land of the Amorites, the Hittites, the Perizzites, the Canaanites, the Hivites and the Jebusites; and I will completely destroy them" (Exod. 23:20–23).

If that were the only time this angel was mentioned in Scripture, it would be important but perhaps not otherwise noteworthy. However, centuries later, another prophet of God revealed specific details in both the person and the work of this angel:

> I shall make mention of the lovingkindnesses of the LORD, the praises of the LORD, according to all that the LORD has granted us, and the great goodness toward the house of Israel, which He has granted them according to His compassion and according to the abundance of His lovingkindnesses. For He said, "Surely, they are My people; sons who will not deal falsely."
>
> So He became their Savior. In all their affliction He was afflicted, *and the angel of His presence saved them*; in His love and in His mercy He redeemed them, and He lifted them and carried them all the days of old.
>
> But they rebelled and grieved His Holy Spirit; therefore He turned Himself to become their enemy, He fought against them (Isa. 63:7–10).

It is crucial to note that this angel became their Savior (Isa. 63:9), and at this particular time before the Incarnation, God's Word described Him in terms that will be used repeatedly in our study because this was not just any angel, this was, literally in the Hebrew "the Angel of His Face" or "the Angel of His Presence." The Hebrew word *paneh* can be translated as either "face" or "presence," and these are virtually interchangeable synonyms in the Hebrew language. This section in Isaiah is also one of the most prominent Old Testament references to the Trinity because all three members are present: God the Father as "the LORD" (Isa. 63:7), this special Angel of His face as their Savior (Isa. 63:8–9), and "the Holy Spirit" (Isa. 63:10).

In the relatively early unveiling of God's progressive revelation, the nation of Israel did not realize the significance of what God had promised by sending His angel in Exodus 23, but the Godhead did—and that was all that mattered. He did not become the Angel of His Face/Presence in Isaiah 63; this Scripture reveals what truly had taken place in Exodus many centuries earlier. Fittingly, after the

Incarnation, there is never again a reference to such an Angel. In fact, it would be a biblical impossibility for another appearance of such an Angel because of the resurrected body that Jesus currently inhabits (Col. 2:9).

So by the time Exodus 23 took place, the Redeemer LORD had accomplished so much. But God had not finished teaching His people in reference to Himself—and to His face.

♦ ♦ ♦ ♦ ♦ ♦ ♦

The Mosaic Covenant was ratified in Exodus 24:1–8, becoming the first bilateral (or "two way") covenant that God had ever made. Previously, in ratifying the Noahic Covenant (Gen. 9:9–17) and the Abrahamic Covenant (Gen. 15:12–21), God alone was the ratifying agent, and this became important because anyone who ratifies the covenants must meet covenant requirements and fulfill covenant obligations. These two previous "covenants of promise" (Eph. 2:12) showed very specific promises of what God was going to do; in this first bilateral covenant, God had a part and the Jewish people had a part. Notice how Exodus 24:7–8 summarizes this: "Then he [Moses] took the book of the covenant and read it in the hearing of the people; and they said, 'All that the LORD has spoken we will do, and we will be obedient!' So Moses took the blood and sprinkled it on the people, and said, 'Behold, the blood of the [Mosaic] covenant, which the LORD has made with you in accordance with all these words.'"

And then, without drawing any attention to it or without introducing it with fanfare, another earth-shattering enigma occurred in the immediate verses that follow:

> Then Moses went up with Aaron, Nadab and Abihu, and seventy of the elders of Israel, *and they saw the God of Israel*; and under His feet there appeared to be a pavement

of sapphire, as clear as the sky itself. Yet He did not stretch out His hand against the nobles of the sons of Israel; *and they saw God*, and they ate and drank (Ex. 24:9–11).

It is not coincidental nor is it haphazardly placed that this totally unexpected encounter with God—especially an encounter with the God who can be seen—occurred immediately after the Mosaic Covenant was ratified—not before it. Previously in Exodus 19:21, God had warned "lest they [the Jewish people] break through to the LORD to gaze, and many of them perish," now He Himself initiated this close assembly, inviting Moses and seventy-three others not only "to see God" (mentioned twice in the text) but also to enjoy a fellowship meal with Him. Seventy-four people ate a communal meal with God, and saw Him—and yet He chose not to destroy them. This communal meal included, at the very least, the staples of the day: bread and wine (cf. Gen. 14:18–20).

Though the Bible offers no dialogue from the participants, such a fellowship with God must have changed these men forever! What a testimony they would have to tell others, unless God restricted them as Jesus would do later after the Transfiguration (Matt. 17:9). This event did not merely transpire randomly; it took place *immediately* following the ratification of the Mosaic Covenant. Or stated another way, no invitation to God's communal meal was given to these representative leaders of Israel until the people were brought into covenant relation and obedience to Him. This eternally life-altering encounter with the visible God must have sparked much conversation and debate among the participants. Even though they did not understand fully, they could deduce that a fellowship meal of bread and wine (and whatever else God served in this meal) is possible in the very presence of God if He so desires and so initiates this. In the unfolding and fuller progression of Scripture, it should not surprise us that God would initiate a communal meal with Him not only in Exodus 24, but also in a much fuller capacity at a later communal meal of bread and wine in the very presence of God at the Last Supper that would occur almost fifteen hundred years later.

We should note one sad observation: this select group had a special, unspeakably gracious audience with the visible God, yet the ones who had seen God fell into grievous sin. For instance, Aaron, the first high priest, who was a part of the communal meal with the God whom he saw, assisted shortly thereafter with fashioning the brazenly wicked Golden Calf idol, as detailed in Exodus 32:1–4:

> Now when the people saw that Moses delayed to come down from the mountain, the people assembled about Aaron, and said to him, "Come, make us a god who will go before us; as for this Moses, the man who brought us up from the land of Egypt, we do not know what has become of him." And Aaron said to them, "Tear off the gold rings which are in the ears of your wives, your sons, and your daughters, and bring them to me."
>
> Then all the people tore off the gold rings which were in their ears, and brought them to Aaron. And he took this from their hand, and fashioned it with a graving tool, and made it into a molten calf; and they said, "This is your god, O Israel, who brought you up from the land of Egypt."

Not too many days afterwards, Aaron's own sons, Nadab and Abihu, also present on the mountain and functioning heirs in the priesthood, would soon offer "strange fire before the LORD" that was unacceptable to God in either what they brought to Him or in the manner in which they brought it—and the LORD responded by immediately killing them with fire:

> Now Nadab and Abihu, the sons of Aaron, took their respective firepans, and after putting fire in them, placed incense on it and offered strange fire before the Lord, which He had not commanded them. And fire came out from the presence of the Lord and consumed them, and they died before the Lord.
>
> Then Moses said to Aaron, "It is what the Lord spoke, saying,
>
> 'By those who come near Me I will be treated as holy, and before all the people I will be honored.'"
>
> So Aaron, therefore, kept silent (Lev. 10:1–3).

In Numbers 13–14, the spies who were sent out to view the land returned with this report, in Numbers 14:36–37: "As for the men whom Moses sent to spy out the land and who returned and made all the congregation grumble against him by bringing out a bad report concerning the land, even those men who brought out the very bad report of the land died by a plague before the Lord." One important biblical truth is often overlooked: none of the elders who had seen God stood with Joshua and Caleb, and all of these elders died in the wilderness with the rest of the sinful nation (Num. 14:26–31). The deaths do not necessarily mean that all of these men, or even any, were eternally lost; but what this example does show will become much clearer with the unfolding revelation of God, "to whom much is given, much is required" (Luke 12:48). So seventy-four men ate a blessed fellowship meal and viewed God, and by God's grace they were not destroyed. But God had much more to offer with His fuller intention involving His face in something that we generally do not associate it with.

♦ ♦ ♦ ♦ ♦ ♦ ♦

As a baby Christian, or perhaps even before I was saved, I, as many others have, purposed to read through the entire Bible, much of which I did not understand, especially when it came to Exodus 25–40, where God instructed Moses how He wanted His Tabernacle (and later His Temple) to be constructed. For me, the Bible changed once I came to Exodus 25, and as far as I was concerned, without many of the modern helps/tools available, changed for the worse. Instead of action stories, including the account of the Flood and the story of Joseph being sold into bondage, these verses were strange, bizarre (to me) instructions. For instance, in Exodus 25:30, my King James Bible told of "shewbread." What in the world was that? Later translations would have "showbread," which made a little more sense to me at that young age, but then again, why would God want this bread shown? I eventually made it through the Book of Exodus, but it was very hard and exceedingly dry for me.

Now having gone to seminary, and in my on-going studies as a Christian and a professor, I have a much better appreciation for what happened. After the Mosaic Covenant was ratified by both God and the Jewish people (Ex. 24:1–8) and the fellowship meal that included viewing God followed (Ex. 24:9–11), God gave commands for the sons of Israel to "construct a sanctuary for Me, that I may dwell among them" (Ex. 25:8). While generally not noticed, this act of God is incredibly gracious. In Genesis 3 God expelled the newly fallen couple from His Holy presence; not until the ratification of the Mosaic Covenant—and for the first time ever recorded in Scripture—would God Himself actually dwell in the very midst of the people, in some ways temporarily reversing what He had done in Genesis 3.

Fittingly, the account beginning in Exodus 25 begins with God—not with the people—as He worked His way out toward His nation. Accordingly, the Ark of the Covenant, which would contain a much needed *mercy* seat, would be the place where God promised: "There I will meet with you; and from above the mercy seat, from between the two cherubim which are upon the ark of the testimony, I will speak to you about all that I will give you in commandment for the sons of Israel" (Ex. 25:22).

Still moving from the vantage point of beginning with God in what would become the Holy of Holies and moving outward, the item that would receive a special place of recognition in the northern-most part of the Holy Place, which the Jews considered a most sacred place: the table of shewbread/showbread. This bread must be vitally important to be placed so close to God in both the Tabernacle and eventually the Temple, where basically the same floor plan was used. While it may not initially make sense to us, the Hebrew translation of what God wanted is much richer in content and explanation: "And you shall set [literally in the Hebrew] the Bread of the Face/the Bread of the Presence [*paneh*] in front of me at all times" (Ex. 25:30). This same designation is also found in Exodus 35:13 and 39:36.

As we saw, the Hebrew word [paneh] is used interchangeably for "face" and "presence." By the way, we do somewhat the same thing in English by using the word "face" to convey sometimes more than just the physical features. For example, "He did it to save face" (that is, to keep from utter embarrassment); "I wonder if he will show his face" (used usually in a negative way to show whether or not someone would have the nerve to show up where he would not be welcome or expected). So the Hebrew word for face was used the same way. It can mean and often does mean someone's literal face, or it can denote a special presence—especially when used of God. The context of the passage often helps to determine which one is a better translation.

So the Bread of the Face carries the very sure designation of "The Bread of God's Presence" or even "The Bread of God's Face." This greatly exceeds the designation of "showbread" in importance. No dialogue between God and Moses exists in this account. If any did occur, it is not recorded in Scripture. Most likely no conversation took place because God was giving directions about the precise design

He wanted in His Tabernacle and ultimately in His own Temple that was necessary for Him—holy, pure, undefiled—to dwell in the very midst of a people who possessed none of these attributes. If Moses had questions, he may have asked God later.

This Bread of the Face would also be called "the continual bread" in a quite warming passage, especially as it relates to the special presence of God, as seen in Numbers 4:7: "Over the table of the bread of the Presence they shall also spread a cloth of blue and put on it the dishes and the pans and the sacrificial bowls and the jars for the libation, and the continual bread shall be on it." This would also be the bread that King David and his men would eat in First Samuel 21:6, of which Jesus referred to in Matthew 12:4 and Luke 6:4. By the strict dictates of the Mosaic Covenant, David and his men were not to eat of this bread (it was designated only for the priests), but their pressing need showed God's gracious condescension in this one particular case by allowing this bread to be consumed. Hebrews 9:2 describes the Bread of the Face as "the sacred bread."

So from an aerial view, looking downward into the Tabernacle, the one-third part on the left would be Holy of Holies, with the Ark of the Covenant and ultimately the Shekinah Glory of God. The outer veil separated the remaining two-thirds of the Tabernacle into the section called the Holy Place. Yet the closest thing to God Himself on the northern side of the Holy Place—yet still outside the veil of separation—was the Bread of His Face/Presence. If you reversed the order and approached God from outside the Tabernacle, the same would be true. The last thing the priests would see on the northern spot deemed sacred in the Holy Place would be the table displaying the Bread of His Face and then the separation caused by the God-mandated veil. What a startling and astonishingly fearful—and so theologically deep—event would occur centuries later, when God Himself ripped open the previously restrictive veil (Matt. 27:51), allowing His own to draw near with confidence to the very presence of God that He Himself had graciously established (Heb. 4:15–16). Understanding the Bread of His Face also makes every "Bread reference" that Jesus made in reference to Himself much richer in meaning. But that would not happen until the Incarnation. In the meantime, under the Mosaic Covenant, all the things associated with the Tabernacle and centuries later the Temple were only "things which are a mere shadow of what is to come; but the substance belongs to Christ [Messiah]" (Col. 2:17).

But before this, God had much to teach a bewildered Moses regarding both Himself and His face.

◆ ◆ ◆ ◆ ◆ ◆

As we saw previously, the Mosaic Covenant was ratified in Exodus 24. From that time until further notice, the nation of Israel lived under its covenantal privileges and responsibilities promising "all that the LORD has spoken we will do, and we will be obedient!" (Ex. 24:7). Very short lived was this promise because in only a few weeks after that, while Moses was receiving further instruction from God, the hard-hearted people approached the one who would be the first high priest of Israel: "Now when the people saw that Moses delayed to come down from the mountain, the people assembled about Aaron and said to him, 'Come, make us a god who will go before us; as for this Moses, the man who brought us up from the land of Egypt, we do not know what has become of him'" (Ex. 32:1). Foolishly, Aaron took their gold and fashioned it into an idol of a golden calf as the people wickedly exclaimed, "This is your god, O Israel, who brought you up from the land of Egypt" (Ex. 32:2–4). In these heinous, brazen covenant violations against Yahweh and the Mosaic Covenant (no other gods; no idols) the people could not claim that they acted in ignorance; this was a high-handed sin of rebellion. Moses' vantage point of what had occurred is given in Exodus 32:21: "Then Moses said to Aaron, 'What did this people do to you, that you have brought such great sin upon them?'" On that same day, Exodus 32:28 reveals that the Levites executed about three thousand men that day. And here is an important item to note: it was *only* by the utter grace of God that Aaron was not removed from being the high priest of Israel, executed with other participants, and replaced by the next of his sons in line for becoming the next high priest.

The brazen sin of the golden calf was not limited only to the ones already mentioned; the sin of Exodus 32 affected the entire nation. After such a high-handed sin, when God removed His presence from the camp as an object lesson to the newly redeemed nation because of their covenant sinfulness (Ex. 33:1–10), a dialogue took place between God and Moses. God had promised to send His angel with Moses and the nation (Ex. 33:2), but He Himself would not go with the people (Ex. 33:3). This terrible news for Moses became the basis for the conversations that follow, all of them ultimately related to the face of God. Each word for "face" or "presence" will be the same Hebrew word that we saw before, *paneh*—and this chapter will add further enigmas.

To begin with, Exodus 33:11 states, "Thus the LORD used to speak to Moses face to face [*paneh* to *paneh*], just as a man speaks to his friend." Moses was still concerned that God's presence would not be with the people, so God promised "My presence [*paneh*] shall go with you, and I will give you rest" (Ex. 33:14). Moses pleaded, "If your presence [*paneh*] does not go up with us, do not lead us from here" (Ex. 33:15). Then Moses—who had seen a visual manifestation of God at the burning bush (Ex. 3), had eaten a fellowship meal with Him on the mountain (Ex. 24:9–11)—knew there was still more. He implored God to "show me Your glory" (Ex. 33:18). God then responded in an initially bewildering way: He informed Moses in Exodus 33:20,

"You cannot see My face [*paneh*], for no man can see me and live!" So in the same chapter where God used to speak to Moses face to face [*paneh* to *paneh*] (Ex. 33:13), God also restricted Moses from seeing His face [*paneh*] (Ex. 33:20). In fact, the chapter concludes by God's promises to place Moses in the cleft of the rock until He passed by, and "then I will take My hand away and you shall see My back, but My face [*paneh*] shall not be seen" (Ex. 33:23).

There is much more to add to this, and we will do so in the upcoming chapters. But if God's revelation ended here, it would leave us tremendously confused. So in summarizing what we have seen in this chapter, the word *face* or *presence* can be used in reference to God in personal form as the Angel of His Face/Presence, or in an inanimate, symbolic form as the Bread of His Face/Presence. But God had much, much richer and fuller explanations to give to untangle these enigmas—and to put the focus on the person and the work of His promised Messiah.

CHAPTER THREE

THE PEACE

For all who have been truly saved since the death and resurrection of the Lord Jesus Christ, God grants us unfathomable spiritual truths, as Romans 5:1–2 give evidence: "Therefore, having been justified by faith, we have peace with God through our Lord Jesus Christ, through whom also we have obtained our introduction by faith into this grace in which we stand; and we exult in hope of the glory of God." Theologians call this a "positional truth," that is, something that is positionally true all of the time once you have received it. Ephesians 1:3 is one of the dozens of such examples of positional truths: "Blessed be the God and Father of our Lord Jesus Christ, who has blessed us with every spiritual blessing in the heavenly places in Christ." Whether we even realized at the time we were saved (most do not realize it; I certainly did not), we are eternally "blessed with *every* spiritual blessing" and are "seated in the heavenly places in Christ" (Eph. 1:20). This is not something that you seek once you are saved; it is a grace gift by-product of being saved.

So back to the astounding positional truth of Romans 5:1: "Therefore, having been justified by faith, *we have peace with God* through our Lord Jesus Christ." This is not a command to seek after peace with God; it is a positional truth already granted to the redeemed. On our best day as a Christian we whom God saved do not deserve this (such is the nature of all of God's grace gifts), and on our worst day as Christians, we do not forfeit these (such is the blessed on-going nature of all of God's positional truths that He freely bestowed on His own). However, just because we receive unspeakable spiritual truths in this lifetime, they certainly do not coincide with the teachings of the "Prosperity Gospel," nor do they necessarily mean an easy life. The verses that follow Romans 5:1-2 clearly reveal this: "And not only this, but we also exult in our tribulations, knowing that tribulation brings about perseverance; and perseverance, proven character; and proven character, hope; and hope does not disappoint, because the love of God has been poured out within our hearts through the Holy Spirit who was given to us" (Rom. 5:3-5).

We should note a couple of disclaimers about these verses. God may very well discipline His children who sin, as Hebrews 12:7 fearfully warns: "It is for discipline that you endure; God deals with you as sons; for what son is there whom his father does not discipline?" But even in this, if you truly are saved, the positional truths never go away in spite of God's disciplining. How God performs this divine disciplining and to what degree, He does not say; God does not allow Himself to be put into a box. However, in this context of Hebrews is also the warning that if you claim to be a Christian, fall into habitual sin and are not disciplined by God, you may indeed not be saved: "But if you are without discipline, of which all have become partakers, then you are illegitimate children and not sons." Such illegitimate children would claim to be saved and thus presume to have all of God's blessings, but by their habitual sin they show that they never were truly saved.

But for those who truly possess positional "peace with God" and are currently walking in obedience to Him, God Himself offers tremendous teachings of comfort when circumstances bombard us and our lives become increasingly tumultuous. While there are many passages that teach about God's peace, a favorite for many (myself included) is Philippians 4:4-9:

Rejoice in the Lord always; again I will say, rejoice! Let your forbearing spirit be known to all men. The Lord is near. Be anxious for nothing, but in everything by prayer and supplication with thanksgiving let your requests be made known to God. And the peace of God, which surpasses all comprehension, shall guard your hearts and your minds in Christ Jesus.

Finally, brethren, whatever is true, whatever is honorable, whatever is right, whatever is pure, whatever is lovely, whatever is of good repute, if there is any excellence and if anything worthy of praise, let your mind dwell on these things.

The things you have learned and received and heard and seen in me, practice these things; and the God of peace shall be with you.

In this final section of Paul's letter to his beloved Philippian brothers and sisters, he employed two different terms: "the peace of God" (Phil. 4:7) and "the God of peace" (Phil. 4:9). The peace of God is what He brings; the God of peace is who He is—and truly you cannot have one without the other. Somewhat similar to "The Agreement" chapter in *The Cup and the Glory*, you do not seek "peace with God;" you implement the commands that God's Word contains in the previous verses. Instead of praying, "Please give me Your peace, God," the commands are to (1) rejoice in the Lord (4:4), (2) again I say rejoice (4:4), which is "faith in action" as you put the focus on God and His sovereignty even when—or especially when—your feelings tell you otherwise. Further, (3) let your forbearing (patient, longsuffering) spirit be made known to all men (4:5), as you again show your faith in action. These are not accomplished by haphazardly trying to psyche yourself up that all will be well, or by wishing it into existence; the ending part of 4:5 reminds us why we should follow His commands: "The Lord is near." There is a debate among scholars whether that is a reference to the return of the Lord (Phil. 3:20–21), or to His very nearness—or a combination of both. Regardless of which Paul intended, the overwhelming truth that loudly calls out from this section is "You, child of God, are never alone."

The final commands in this section follow: (4) be anxious for nothing (not "be anxious for only one third of things"), (5) but in *everything* by prayer and supplication *with thanksgiving* (*before* God intervenes and brings about His remedy, thanking God that He is there and His ways are right), (6) let your requests be made to God (Phil. 4:6). With these six components implemented on a daily basis, you have God's promise: "And *the peace of God*, which passes all comprehension shall guard your hearts [your emotions/volition] and minds [your thoughts] in Christ Jesus" (Phil. 4:7). Notice that this actually is not a request for God's peace; instead He brings His peace for those who do these things. Also, notice that there truly is no peace of God without the closeness of the Person of God. Many people expect their circumstances to change; God calls His children first and foremost to focus on Him.

In the same section of Philippians and just as important are the commands that immediately follow. These are our responsibilities as Christians—not God's—to have as an active part of our lives. In regard to the mind, Philippians 4:8 commands: "Finally, brethren, whatever is true, whatever is honorable, whatever is right, whatever is pure, whatever is lovely, whatever is of good repute, if there is any excellence and if anything worthy of praise, let your mind dwell on these things." Note how the verse ends: "let your mind dwell on these things." It is important to understand that this is a present tense verb, which could be translated, "Let your mind continually on a non-stop basis dwell on these things." Philippians 4:9 concludes this section: "The things you have learned and received and heard and seen in me, practice these things, and the God of peace will be with you." The verb used here means that instead of just thinking on these things (4:8), it is the faith-in-action doing or practicing these things. As with the verb ending in 4:7, this is a present tense verb that could be rendered "continuously on a non-stop basis practice these things."

And with all of these implemented on an on-going basis, beginning in Philippians 4:4 and continuing through 4:9, look at God's marvelous promise as He concludes: "the God of peace shall be with you." Go back sometime and think through the ramifications that these verses teach. There is no true peace of God without doing what He commands us to do; there is no sense of understanding the very God of peace without doing these. This is why I stated earlier that we are not to pray so much for God's peace about the circumstances which cause us burden; instead, we are "to draw near to Him," as is found in a section that virtually mirrors First Peter 5:1–10. We think in regard to our hard circumstances; God thinks in terms of our relationship and walk with Him. Finally, it should be understood that for many of these commands, God requires that we do them in private with Him alone. It is fine to tell brothers and sisters in Christ about certain matters in our lives and about certain prayer concerns, but all that God commands in this section has to do with your one-on-one walk with God.

What wonderful promises God gives for those who are saved in Christ Jesus!

But what if you are a believer who lived before the birth of the Messiah, and did so in the midst of a nation that lived in utter covenant disobedience to God?

♦ ♦ ♦ ♦ ♦ ♦ ♦

When God brought the nation of Israel into being a unique functioning nation before Him with the ratification of the Mosaic Covenant (Ex. 24:1–8), He gave the Jewish people a crystal-clear proposition: Obey Me and I will greatly bless you in every area of your life; disobey Me and I will equally curse you in every area of your life. This was an "either-or proposition;" no middle ground existed. Later, God gave specifics in what this meant in the blessing section of Leviticus 26:1–13. Among other blessings, we should note two very important ones. The first one regarded the crops, which of course meant that God had to provide the necessary rain. Here is God's promise to the nation of Israel in Leviticus 26:3–5: "If you walk in My statutes and keep My commandments so as to carry them out, then I shall give you rains in their season, so that the land will yield its produce and the trees of the field will bear their fruit. Indeed, your threshing will last for you until grape gathering, and grape gathering will last until sowing time. You will thus eat your food to the full and live securely in your land." The second one promised that if the nation walked in covenant obedience before Yahweh, her enemies would be routinely defeated: "I shall also grant peace in the land, so that you may lie down with no one making you tremble. I shall also eliminate harmful beasts from the land, and no sword will pass through your land. But you will chase your enemies, and they will fall before you by the sword; five of you will chase a hundred, and a hundred of you will chase ten thousand, and your enemies will fall before you by the sword" (Lev. 26:6–8).

However, the curse section of Leviticus 26:14–39 was just as valid and binding on the newly redeemed Jewish people as the blessing section had been, as God clearly explained the consequences of disobedience to Him before they happened. For the Jewish nation, disobedience would result in famine: "If also after these things, you do not obey Me, then I will punish you seven times more for your sins. And I will also break down your pride of power; I will also make your sky like iron and your earth like bronze. And your strength shall be spent uselessly, for your land shall not yield its produce and the trees of the land shall not yield their fruit" (Lev. 26:18–20). In the statement before these verses, God promised strong judgment by allowing Israel's enemies to defeat them: "I will set My face [*paneh*] against you so that you will be struck down before your enemies; and those who hate you will rule over you, and you will flee when no one is pursuing you" (Lev. 26:17). The core problem would not be a change in the weather, nor a flawed military strategy; the core problem would be the national sinful rebellion against God.

Similar to Leviticus 26, Deuteronomy 28 offered the nation either God's blessing (28:1–14) or His cursing (28:15–68), with each part directly related to whether or not the nation walked in obedience to Him. This section eventually became known as a unit entitled "the blessing and the curse" (Deut. 30:1) (which greatly differs from the generic *a* blessing and *a* curse in general). Although not at all limited just to this, the same two items previously seen in Leviticus 26 are written here as well: namely, abundance of harvest (Deut. 28:5,8) or drought (28:23–24), and military victory for obedience (Deut. 28:7) or utter defeat due to national disobedience (Deut. 28:25). God offered no middle ground for them because such is the nature of true obedience.

Technically speaking, this section of Scripture has nothing to do with America or any other nation. It is part of the covenant blessings and responsibilities that God made with the Jewish people under the Mosaic Covenant at Mount Sinai. Also, from this point forward, "the blessing and the curse" becomes a spiritual barometer for how the nation of Israel was doing in its relationship—even more to the point, its obedience—to God. If Israel won a military battle, such as at Jericho in Joshua 6, the nation as a whole was living in covenant obedience to God. When the nation sinned against God, they were defeated in battle at Ai, a much lesser village (Josh. 7). Go through the rest of Old Testament and you will find this repeatedly demonstrated. As shown in a chapter of *The Bible Expositor's Handbook* (OT), young David, in covenant obedience to Yahweh, slew Goliath (1 Sam. 17).

Contrary to its use in sporting events as a description of the underdog defeating a much stronger foe, David defeating Goliath is not an upset; this should be expected, as *God's faithfulness* to His covenant promises are demonstrated again and again and again.

For example, Ruth 1:1 states that there was a famine in the land. This verse by itself gives testimony that the Jews as a whole were not living in obedience to Yahweh at that time, or there would have been no famine. A faithful remnant walked in obedience, but the majority did not, and God punished the nation precisely as He had repeatedly promised that He would.

With this background, the Book of Judges reads true to form. Judges 2 begins with an appearance by God Himself as the Angel of the LORD who spoke for God and His covenant faithfulness and rebuked the nation for their disobedience:

> Now the angel of the LORD came up from Gilgal to Bochim. And he said, "I brought you up out of Egypt and led you into the land which I have sworn to your fathers; and I said, 'I will never break My covenant with you, and as for you, you shall make no covenant with the inhabitants of this land; you shall tear down their altars.' But you have not obeyed Me; what is this you have done? Therefore I also said, 'I will not drive them out before you; but they will become as thorns in your sides and their gods will be a snare to you.'"
>
> When the angel of the LORD spoke these words to all the sons of Israel, the people lifted up their voices and wept. So they named that place Bochim; and there they sacrificed to the LORD (Jud. 2:1–5).

A summary statement of the faithfulness during Joshua's generation followed by the wickedness of the subsequent generations follows next in Judges 2:6–10:

> When Joshua had dismissed the people, the sons of Israel went each to his inheritance to possess the land. And the people served the LORD all the days of Joshua, and all the days of the elders who survived Joshua, who had seen all the great work of the LORD which He had done for Israel. Then Joshua the son of Nun, the servant of the LORD, died at the age of one hundred and ten. And they buried him in the territory of his inheritance in Timnath-heres, in the hill country of Ephraim, north of Mount Gaash. And all that generation also were gathered to their fathers; and there arose another generation after them who did not know the LORD, nor yet the work which He had done for Israel.

In just these verses, based on the blessing and the curse section of Leviticus 26 and Deuteronomy 28, God had already announced how He would respond unless the people truly repented and put themselves into covenant obedience. Accordingly, it is not surprising that the theological analysis and description of the terrible times of the judges is given next. Nothing in this section happened by coincidence; everything was a divinely mandated cause and effect, as shown in Judges 2:11–23:

> Then the sons of Israel did evil in the sight of the LORD, and served the Baals, and they forsook the LORD, the God of their fathers, who had brought them out of the land of Egypt, and followed other gods from among the

gods of the peoples who were around them, and bowed themselves down to them; thus they provoked the Lord to anger. So they forsook the Lord and served Baal and the Ashtaroth. And the anger of the Lord burned against Israel, and He gave them into the hands of plunderers who plundered them; and He sold them into the hands of their enemies around them, so that they could no longer stand before their enemies. Wherever they went, the hand of the Lord was against them for evil, as the Lord had spoken and as the Lord had sworn to them, so that they were severely distressed.

Then the Lord raised up judges who delivered them from the hands of those who plundered them. And yet they did not listen to their judges, for they played the harlot after other gods and bowed themselves down to them. They turned aside quickly from the way in which their fathers had walked in obeying the commandments of the Lord; they did not do as their fathers. And when the Lord raised up judges for them, the Lord was with the judge and delivered them from the hand of their enemies all the days of the judge; for the Lord was moved to pity by their groaning because of those who oppressed and afflicted them. But it came about when the judge died, that they would turn back and act more corruptly than their fathers, in following other gods to serve them and bow down to them; they did not abandon their practices or their stubborn ways.

So the anger of the Lord burned against Israel, and He said, "Because this nation has transgressed My covenant which I commanded their fathers, and has not listened to My voice, I also will no longer drive out before them any of the nations which Joshua left when he died, in order to test Israel by them, whether they will keep the way of the LORD to walk in it as their fathers did, or not." So the LORD allowed those nations to remain, not driving them out quickly; and He did not give them into the hand of Joshua.

Within this background, Judges 6 occurs. The chapter begins by noting the nation of Israel's direct disobedience to God and His subsequent harsh treatment of them at the hands of their enemies, as would be expected from Leviticus 26/Deuteronomy 28 and Judges 2. As always, the problem was not that a foreign invader attacked; the problem was the rebellious hearts and actions of most of the nation that led to God's promised judgment. Judges 6:1–10 should not be surprising:

> Then the sons of Israel did what was evil in the sight of the LORD; and the LORD gave them into the hands of Midian seven years. The power of Midian prevailed against Israel. Because of Midian the sons of Israel made for themselves the dens which were in the mountains and the caves and the strongholds. For it was when Israel had sown, that the Midianites would come up with the Amalekites and the sons of the east and go against them. So they would camp against them and destroy the produce of the earth as far as Gaza, and leave no sustenance in Israel as well as no sheep, ox, or donkey. For they would come up with their livestock and their tents, they would come in like locusts for number, both they and their camels were innumerable; and they came into the land to devastate it. So Israel was brought very low because of Midian, and the sons of Israel cried to the LORD.

Now it came about when the sons of Israel cried to the LORD on account of Midian, that the LORD sent a prophet to the sons of Israel, and he said to them, "Thus says the LORD, the God of Israel, 'It was I who brought you up from Egypt and brought you out from the house of slavery. I delivered you from the hands of the Egyptians and from the hands of all your oppressors, and dispossessed them before you and gave you their land, and I said to you, "I am the LORD your God; you shall not fear the gods of the Amorites in whose land you live. But you have not obeyed Me.""

It is in this context, Gideon emerges: "Then the angel of the LORD came and sat under the oak that was in Ophrah, which belonged to Joash the Abiezrite as his son Gideon was beating out wheat in the wine press in order to save it from the Midianites. The angel of the LORD appeared to him and said to him, "The LORD is with you, O valiant warrior" (Jud. 6:11–12). Two points of interest should be noted: (1) Gideon's meager amount of grain required only a small winepress, and (2) the task to save wheat from the enemies was generally not that of "valiant warriors." Obviously, God knew what Gideon could and would become and how he would be used of God if he—unlike the nation—walked in obedience to God.

We do not know the timeframe between Judges 2 and Judges 6. Gideon may have been present when the Angel of the LORD appeared to rebuke the nation, or he may have heard about God's denunciation later. But regardless of when it was, it did not make much of an impression on Gideon because he initially blamed God for their present problems: "Then Gideon said to him, "O my lord, if the LORD is with us, why then has all this happened to us? And where are all His miracles which our fathers told us about, saying, 'Did not the LORD bring us up from Egypt?' But now the LORD has abandoned us and given us into the hand of Midian" (Jud. 6:13). Interestingly, God started with "The LORD is with you," but Gideon viewed God as having abandoned the Jewish nation. God then commissioned Gideon to lead the people against the Midianites. Actually, every judge that God raised up and commissioned was an act of grace and covenant faithfulness on His part.

You can read the remainder of the story on your own in Judges 6:14–20, but for our study, the verses beginning with Judges 6:21 are important. In reference to the sign that Gideon had sought and the offering that he had brought before God, the following occurred: "Then the angel of the LORD put out the end of the staff that was in his hand and touched the meat and the unleavened bread; and fire sprang up from the rock and consumed the meat and the unleavened bread. Then the angel of the LORD vanished from his sight." Gideon immediately realized his severe predicament, as Judges 6:22 reveals: "When Gideon saw that he was the angel of the LORD, he said, 'Alas, O Lord GOD! For now I have seen the angel of the LORD face to face [*paneh* to *paneh*].'" Notice that God did not correct Gideon by saying, "No, you have not!" Gideon actually had seen the face of God. Gideon fully expected to die, but God instead graciously responded: "The LORD said to him, 'Peace to you, do not fear; you shall not die'" (Jud. 6:23). This most face-to-face encounter made a lasting impression on Gideon, as it did with everyone else described in the Bible accounts of their having seen the face of God.

Gideon marked the occasion then and for all people who would come in the future: "Then Gideon built an altar there to the LORD and named it 'The LORD is Peace.' To this day it is still in Ophrah of the Abiezrites" (Jud. 6:24). *Yahweh shalom*—"The LORD is Peace." What a beautiful name and title for God. Notice how similar it is to later revelation given by God later in Philippians 4: "The LORD is Peace"—not only that the LORD gives peace—which He does—but rather the emphasis is that the Lord *is* peace. God brought the young judge into a deeper understanding of Himself before He commissioned Gideon for a specific activity. God did not train Gideon to do a task; He brought Gideon near to Himself so that he would become the valiant-warrior vessel that God wanted. Relationship with God—not religious activity—was the hallmark of this encounter with Yahweh-shalom.

And if Gideon had known his Bible, he would have known that God had already brought about this same type of encounter decades earlier with his ancestors of the wilderness generation after the Mosaic Covenant was ratified.

♦ ♦ ♦ ♦ ♦ ♦ ♦

So much had transpired from God's keeping an aspect of His promise by redeeming His Jewish people out of bondage in Egypt (Gen. 15:13–15; Ex. 2:24–25, 3:7–8, and Ex. 12). Three months later, God brought His people to Sinai (Ex. 19:1), and this is important because not only would it be the place where He gave the Ten Commandments (Ex. 20), ratified the Mosaic Covenant (Ex. 24:1–8), and participated in the communal meal of fellowship for Moses and seventy-three others, where twice the text informs us that they saw God (Ex. 24:9–11), but also that Sinai would be the place where the nation stayed until about a third into the Book of Numbers.

We see this place and the timeframe in the text. The entire book of Leviticus, that gives directions about the various offerings, instructions for the priesthood and their helpers the Levites, and the annual feasts, was written at Sinai, as the last verse in the chapter shows: "These are the commandments which the LORD commanded Moses for the sons of Israel at Mount Sinai" (Lev. 27:34). This is likewise true for the Book of Numbers, whose Hebrew title is "In the Wilderness" taken from a word within the opening verse: "Then the LORD spoke to Moses in the wilderness of Sinai, in the tent of meeting, on the first of the second month, in the second year after they had come out of the land of Egypt " (Num. 1:1). The timeframe given shows that only one year and one month had transpired since the Exodus—all at Mount Sinai. Finally, twenty days after Numbers 1:1, the nation eventually departed, as Numbers 10:11–12 shows: "Now in the second year, in the second month, on the twentieth of the month, the cloud was lifted from over the tabernacle of the testimony; and the sons of Israel set out on their journeys from the wilderness of Sinai. Then the cloud settled down in the wilderness of Paran." So much had happened, both good and bad, by the time Numbers 10:11 took place—and all the bad directly originated from the people's sin.

It would seem that instead of any kind of loving relationship with Yahweh, all He wanted to do was to attack and destroy, being the angry God that He was (according to many critics of God and His Word). Three thousand were slain after the Golden Calf rebellion (Ex. 32:28). Two potential heirs to becoming the High Priest of Israel were slain because their offering was not in accord with God's instruction (Lev. 10:1–2). Eventually, twelve spies would be sent out to preview the Promised Land, yet ten of them would give a "very bad report to the people" (Num. 14:36–37), and the people longed to return to Egypt after they had rejected God and His chosen leaders Moses and Aaron (Num. 14:1–10). Yet these sinful acts were only a sampling of their disobedience; much more sin took place according to God's perspective. Even though Moses interceded for the sinful nation, God promised the following in Numbers 14:20–24:

> So the LORD said, "I have pardoned them according to your word; but indeed, as I live, all the earth will be filled with the glory of the LORD. Surely all the men who have seen My glory and My signs, which I performed in Egypt and in the wilderness, yet have put Me to the test these ten times and have not listened to My voice, shall by no means see the land which I swore to their fathers, nor shall any

of those who spurned Me see it. But My servant Caleb, because he has had a different spirit and has followed Me fully, I will bring into the land which he entered, and his descendants shall take possession of it.

In the same chapter, God referred to this people as an evil generation and decreed what would take place:

> The LORD spoke to Moses and Aaron, saying, "How long shall I bear with this evil congregation who are grumbling against Me? I have heard the complaints of the sons of Israel, which they are making against Me. Say to them, 'As I live,' says the LORD, 'just as you have spoken in My hearing, so I will surely do to you; your corpses will fall in this wilderness, even all your numbered men, according to your complete number from twenty years old and upward, who have grumbled against Me. Surely you shall not come into the land in which I swore to settle you, except Caleb the son of Jephunneh and Joshua the son of Nun (Num. 14:26–30).

And yet in keeping with the second part of His promise to bring the people back in the fourth generation to the place where He had ratified the Abrahamic Covenant in Genesis 15:16, God further promised in Numbers 14:31–35:

> "Your children, however, whom you said would become a prey—I will bring them in, and they will know the land which you have rejected. But as for you, your corpses will fall in this wilderness. Your sons shall be shepherds for forty years in the wilderness, and they will suffer for your unfaithfulness, until your corpses lie in the wilderness. According

to the number of days which you spied out the land, forty days, for every day you shall bear your guilt a year, even forty years, and you will know My opposition.

"I, the Lord, have spoken, surely this I will do to all this evil congregation who are gathered together against Me. In this wilderness they shall be destroyed, and there they will die."

Sometime at your leisure, go back and trace the reasons for God's strong punitive measures. Every one of these directly relates to at least one blatant covenant violation of God's Mosaic Covenant in the blessing and the curse section of Leviticus 26/Deuteronomy 28. Each one is a reaction to the people's sin, not some arbitrary "lightning bolt from heaven" to judge the people. Every instance demonstrates one particular attribute of God's character that the people then—and many people now and throughout the ages—do not like, accept, or understand: God's utter holiness.

Yet still in the midst of this, none of these judgments were God's original design or desire. He sought to dwell among the people (Ex. 25:8), to meet with them above the Mercy Seat in the Ark of His Covenant (Ex. 25:20–22), and even more astounding, to consecrate His dwelling by His own glory (Ex. 29:43). Simply put, as He would eventually reiterate centuries later in Jeremiah 30:22 and so many other places in His Word: "And you shall be My people, and I will be your God."

Even more to the point is one particular instance of God's original desire. Before the nation left Mount Sinai after one year and twenty days (Num. 10:11), and before the spies were sent out and the people again rebelled against God for the tenth time in their very short history of redemption (Num. 13–14), in such a theologically rich passage, the kindness of God's original design and intention are clearly seen in a blessing that He Himself desired for His people:

Then the Lord spoke to Moses, saying, "Speak to Aaron and to his sons, saying, 'Thus you shall bless the sons of Israel. You shall say to them:

The Lord bless you, and keep you;

The Lord make His face shine on you, and be gracious to you;

The Lord lift up His countenance on you, and give you peace.'

"So they shall invoke My name on the sons of Israel, and I then will bless them." (Num. 6:22–27)

Scholars erroneously call this "Aaron's Blessing" or "The Aaronic Blessing." Obviously, Aaron as the nation's first High Priest and his subsequent heirs would play an important part by God's original design in instilling this blessing, but even a casual reading shows that God is the one who will bless, with His name "The Lord" beginning each of the three lines of blessing. Also, each of the three lines contains two component parts resulting in a total of six combined elements of God's blessing. Twice, the blessings that God intended for the people relates directly to His face. "The Lord make His face [*paneh*] shine on you" (Num. 6:25), followed by "The Lord lift up His countenance [*paneh*] upon you; and give you peace." Perhaps we are surprised when we first consider this blessing that God lifts up His face—not their faces—upon them. Actually, this is indeed a wonderful blessing because it demonstrates God's active and personal care and attention—and desire—to bless those who live in covenant obedience to Him, at this point in the context Jewish, but later also for the Gentiles, as His holy Word would repeatedly show.

No, this is not "Aaron's Blessing"—this is *the Lord's blessing* because it involves (twice) "His face." Or to reason differently, take away God's face and there will be no blessing. As we saw with Philippians 4, God includes Himself with the peace that He alone can give. So as stated before, these are not impersonal blessings that would merely happen; these are direct consequences of Yahweh's offering these promised blessings. As James 1:17 would later plainly show, "Every good thing given and every perfect gift is from above, coming down from the Father of lights, with whom there is no variation or shifting shadow"—all emerging from a true relationship with Him.

Although these verses are used at many weddings or are frequently displayed in believers' homes as plaques or in framed cross-stitched items, as is so often the case, most times they are incomplete. Very few people quote or display the connected verse that is just as inspired, just as binding, and just as mandatory, namely Numbers 6:27: "So they shall invoke My name on the sons of Israel, and I then will bless them." All of the previous items involved the name of the LORD. It is only after God's name was properly invoked that the promise "and I will *then* bless them" would occur. It reasons that without the proper invoking of God's name, He would withhold these connected blessings until the Jewish nation did properly invoke His name in accordance with the stated command.

This mandated invocation of God's name is very personal with God and again is part of His original desire and design. So in descending order, note what this famous blessing entails: "The LORD" (three times), "His face" (twice) and "His name" (once). Remove any of these items—or add to them—and they are no longer God's blessings, but they are reduced to something much less. And tragically, removing God's name is exactly what the Jewish nation eventually did.

CHAPTER FOUR

THE NAME

The word "name" in the Bible can be used in two very distinct ways. In a general sense, it can mean the given name for someone, but when used especially in relation to God, it can depict certain attributes or activities associated with Him. It is not so much a matter that He reveals His name—which is important—but rather that His name often became a means of revealing His divine attributes and His subsequent work uniquely related to Him.

We repeatedly see this in Scripture. For example, in Acts 16:18, Paul cast out the demon from a fortune telling girl by declaring, "I command you in the name of Jesus Christ to come out of her!" This was not just the verbal pronouncement of "Jesus Christ;" "the name" again included divine attributes—such as the power and authority over this evil demonic realm. Paul possessed no power of his own and using "the name" was not learned behavior; he merely exercised the authority granted to him as an apostle in "the name of Jesus Christ." In the Acts 16 context Paul was at Philippi, and years later when he wrote to his beloved Philippian church, he again invoked the importance of the name of Jesus in a passage familiar to many:

> For this reason also, God highly exalted Him, and bestowed on Him the name which is above every name, so that at the name of Jesus every knee will bow, of those who are in heaven and on earth and under the earth, and that every

tongue will confess that Jesus Christ is Lord, to the glory of God the Father (Phil. 2:9–11).

Note the different realm and wide sweep that His name has authority over and what will take place one day in the future. Literally every being created, both human and demonic, saved and unsaved, will one day bow at the name of Jesus. How different Acts 16 and Philippians 2 would be if the name of Jesus Christ were removed, restricted or not used. What would have happened to the demon if Paul had said, "I command you in the name of _____ to come out of her?" The demon would not have budged because no authoritative name would have been used. No account has ever occurred where God rebuked this ex-Pharisee rabbi (Phil. 3:4–5), who freely used the names of God as God had revealed them in Scripture. What folly would be in what people call the Great Commission, if any part of the name were omitted: "baptizing them in the name of _____, and the Son, and _____." By the way, just one small point in passing: Matthew 28:19 is one of the better verses to support the Trinity because it is "name" singular—not "names"—and yet "name" encompasses all three members of the Godhead.

The phrase "the name of the LORD" occurs over one hundred times in Scripture. For the Jewish people and in the Hebrew language and later with the Greek language, the name—especially in reference to God—had more than just a distinguishing title associated with it. The names of God depict His divine nature and character and often demonstrated how He related to His people. Micah 4:5 is one of the many examples of this. In writing about a future time of blessing when the Messiah reigns, Micah wrote "Though all the peoples walk each in the name of his god, as for us, we will walk in the name of the LORD our God forever and ever."

Repeatedly throughout Scripture, God made His name known, and many times He gave the significance of that particular name. In

Deuteronomy 28:58–59, in the curse section of that chapter, God warned: "If you are not careful to observe all the words of this law which are written in this book, to fear this honored and awesome name, the LORD your God, then the LORD will bring extraordinary plagues on you and your descendants, even severe and lasting plagues, and miserable and chronic sicknesses." In a more positive vein, when Moses encountered God at the burning bush, the following dialogue about the name of God took place:

> Then Moses said to God, "Behold, I am going to the sons of Israel, and I will say to them, 'The God of your fathers has sent me to you.' Now they may say to me, 'What is His name?' What shall I say to them?" God said to Moses, "I AM WHO I AM"; and He said, "Thus you shall say to the sons of Israel, 'I AM has sent me to you.'"
>
> God, furthermore, said to Moses, "Thus you shall say to the sons of Israel, 'The LORD, the God of your fathers, the God of Abraham, the God of Isaac, and the God of Jacob, has sent me to you.' This is My name forever, and this is My memorial-name to all generations.
>
> "Go and gather the elders of Israel together and say to them, 'The LORD, the God of your fathers, the God of Abraham, Isaac and Jacob, has appeared to me, saying, "I am indeed concerned about you and what has been done to you in Egypt. So I said, I will bring you up out of the affliction of Egypt to the land of the Canaanite and the Hittite and the Amorite and the Perizzite and the Hivite and the Jebusite, to a land flowing with milk and honey"'" (Ex. 3:13–17).

God did not rebuke Moses for His question regarding God's name, nor would God have reprimanded Moses for using the name "YHWH" or "Yahweh," generally understood to be based on the Hebrew verb "to be:" Yahweh "is who He is."

A few chapters later in Exodus 6:2–6, God revealed the significance of His name Yahweh:

> God spoke further to Moses and said to him, "I am the LORD [Yahweh]; and I appeared to Abraham, Isaac, and Jacob, as God Almighty [El Shaddai], but by My name, LORD [Yahweh], I did not make Myself known to them.
>
> "And I also established My covenant with them, to give them the land of Canaan, the land in which they sojourned. And furthermore I have heard the groaning of the sons of Israel, because the Egyptians are holding them in bondage; and I have remembered My covenant.
>
> "Say, therefore, to the sons of Israel, 'I am the LORD [Yahweh], and I will bring you out from under the burdens of the Egyptians, and I will deliver you from their bondage. I will also redeem you with an outstretched arm and with great judgments.

Because of this passage, the name Yahweh often refers to the covenant-keeping name—and attribute—of God. Also, most scholars conclude that the Patriarchs knew the name of Yahweh because of such passages as "people called on the name of the LORD [Yahweh]" in Genesis 4:26. Exodus 6 emphasizes that God did not previously demonstrate His covenant-keeping aspect of Yahweh as He was now doing in bringing about not only the redemption of the Jewish people from slavery, but also, as we have seen, being true to His covenant promise of bringing Israel to the land He had sworn to give them as an everlasting possession, He had to bring them into relation with Himself (Gen. 15:12–21; 17:7–8; Ex. 2:24–25).

It is essential to mark that God associated His name with His dwelling both in His Tabernacle and later in His Temple. Even before ratifying the Mosaic Covenant in Exodus 24:1–8, while still at Sinai, but in keeping with His desire to dwell among the people (Ex. 25:8), God stated this in Exodus 20:24: "You shall make an altar of earth for Me, and you shall sacrifice on it your burnt offerings and your peace offerings, your sheep and your oxen; in every place where I cause My name to be remembered, I will come to you and bless you." This would be true for His Tabernacle, as Deuteronomy 12:5–7 shows: "But you shall seek the Lord at the place which the Lord your God will choose from all your tribes, to establish His name there for His dwelling, and there you shall come. There you shall bring your burnt offerings, your sacrifices, your tithes, the contribution of your hand, your votive offerings, your freewill offerings, and the firstborn of your herd and of your flock. There also you and your households shall eat before the Lord your God, and rejoice in all your undertakings in which the Lord your God has blessed you."

Specifically in reference to God's Temple, with its more permanent nature, many Scriptures exist that associate God's Temple with His name. We will look at mere samples; many other Scriptures teach the same thing. At the dedication of God's Temple, Solomon stated, "Blessed be the Lord, the God of Israel, who spoke with His mouth to my father David and has fulfilled it with His hand, saying, 'Since the day that I brought My people Israel from Egypt, I did not choose a city out of all the tribes of Israel in which to build a house that My name might be there, but I chose David to be over My people Israel'" (1 Kings 8:15–16). Again in 1 Kings 8:28–29, Solomon prayed, "Yet have regard to the prayer of Your servant and to his supplication, O Lord my God, to listen to the cry and to the prayer which Your servant prays before You today; that Your eyes may be open toward this house night and day, toward the place of which You have said, 'My name shall be there,' to listen to the prayer which Your servant shall pray toward this place." Even more important is how God responded in 1 Kings 9:3: "The LORD said to him, "I have heard your prayer and your supplication, which you have made before Me; I have consecrated this house which you have built *by putting My name there forever*, and My eyes and My heart will be there." It is one thing for Solomon to make the prayer; it is another for God to agree to answer, and He did so by promising to put His name with His Temple forever.

Later, when Israel repeatedly rebelled against Yahweh and lived in covenant disobedience before Him, but before He exiled them in keeping with the curses of Leviticus 26 and Deuteronomy 28, God had much to say regarding His Temple and His Name. As before, these are only a small sample of many verses, but Jeremiah 7 contains many such references. To a wicked, hard-hearted nation who would relatively soon be horrendously judged, pillaged, and exiled, God instructed His prophet Jeremiah:

> The word that came to Jeremiah from the LORD, saying, "Stand in the gate of the LORD's house and proclaim there this word, and say, 'Hear the word of the LORD, all you of Judah, who enter by these gates to worship the LORD!'"
> Thus says the LORD of hosts, the God of Israel, "Amend your ways and your deeds, and I will let you dwell in this place. Do not trust in deceptive words, saying, 'This is the temple of the LORD, the temple of the LORD, the temple of the LORD'" (Jer. 7:1–4).

In a verse familiar to many New Testament readers, God rebuked His sinfully sick nation for their treatment of His own house: "Has this house, which is called by My name, become a den of robbers in your sight? Behold, I, even I, have seen it," declares the LORD" (Jer. 7:11).

Before the Temple was built, the Ark resided at a place called Shiloh. While this should have been a high honor that would accompany God's favor and blessing, instead, because of their great sinfulness centuries before, God judged the place so severely that when God told the people to go to Shiloh, all they would have seen at that time was ruins. Note again how God associates this with His name. In Jeremiah 7:12, God warned the people, "But go now to My place which was in Shiloh, where I made My name dwell at the first, and see what I did to it because of the wickedness of My people Israel." God further warned, "Therefore, I will do to the house which is called by My name, in which you trust, and to the place which I gave you and your fathers, as I did to Shiloh" (Jer. 7:14). In a divine summary assessment of the wickedness the people had done to His own Temple, He charged, "For the sons of Judah have done that which is evil in My sight," declares the LORD, "they have set their detestable things in the house which is called by My name, to defile it" (Jer. 7:30).

Jeremiah 31:35 has this self-declaration from God, highlighting a few of His attributes:

> Thus says the LORD,
> Who gives the sun for light by day,
> And the fixed order of the moon and the stars for
> light by night,
> Who stirs up the sea so that its waves roar;
> The LORD of hosts is His name."

With all these warnings and many, many more, and with the severe curse judgments that God promised in Leviticus 26 and Deuteronomy 28, it would seem extremely unlikely that the Jewish people would somehow ever lose the name of God.

But that is precisely what they did.

♦ ♦ ♦ ♦ ♦ ♦

When the Pharisees confronted Jesus about His disciples not observing the tradition of the elders that had been passed down for centuries, He countered by denouncing them and their tradition—especially their futile attempts to elevate their tradition on par with God's Word:

> Then some Pharisees and scribes came to Jesus from Jerusalem, saying, "Why do Your disciples transgress the tradition of the elders? For they do not wash their hands when they eat bread."
> And He answered and said to them, "And why do you yourselves transgress the commandment of God for the sake of your tradition? For God said, 'Honor your father and mother,' and, 'He who speaks evil of father or mother, let him be put to death.' But you say, 'Whoever shall say to his father or mother, "Anything of mine you might have been helped by has been given to God," he is not to honor his father or his mother.' And thus you invalidated the word of God for the sake of your tradition.
> "You hypocrites, rightly did Isaiah prophesy of you, saying, 'This people honors Me with their lips, but their heart is far away from Me. But in vain do they worship Me, teaching as doctrines the precepts of men'" (Matt. 15:1–9).

Jesus clearly underlined the core theological issues: (1) the Pharisees and scribes were guilty of transgressing the commandment of God for the sake of their man-made tradition (Matt. 15:3), (2) they invalidated the Word of God for the sake of their tradition (Matt. 15:6) and (3) even worse, as Isaiah 29:13 said, not only did they not truly worship the true God—which, of course, they thought they did, and they would be highly insulted by what Jesus was saying to them—they also continually taught "as doctrines the precepts of men" (Matt. 15:9).

Their religious tradition that was developed, codified, and tediously studied by the rabbis over the centuries differed substantially from Deuteronomy 8:3 "Man shall not live by bread alone, but on every word that proceeds out of the mouth of God"—*not* "the mouth of man"—quoted by Jesus in Matthew 4:4 during the forty-day temptation. In Joshua 1:7 God had instructed: "Only be strong and very courageous; be careful to do according to all the law which Moses My servant commanded you; do not turn from it to the right or to the left, so that you may have success wherever you go." "Turning to the right or left" would be the equivalent of not adding anything to God's Word or not taking anything away from it, as God had previously commanded in Deuteronomy 4:2: "You shall not add to the word which I am commanding you, nor take away from it that you may keep the commandments of the LORD your God which I command you." Additionally, in Deuteronomy 5:32, God had already commanded: "So you shall observe to do just as the LORD your God has commanded you; you shall not turn aside to the right or to the left." Joshua thus responded in simple obedience to this command already given as part of the Mosaic Covenant; however, as later Scripture repeatedly shows, many people did not obey.

Paul encountered in essence the same problem in the Greek/Roman world. Writing to the tiny, tucked away church at Colossae, Paul warned the faithful of the same core issues of which Jesus had previously warned in a Jewish setting in Matthew 15, "See to it that no one takes you captive through philosophy and empty deception, according to the tradition of men, according to the elementary principles of the world, rather than according to Christ" (Col. 2:8). That is the introductory sentence of this section. Someone can be taken captive or imprisoned by these philosophical teachings done in God's name, but at their core they were only "the tradition of men," be that of either of Jewish rabbis or Gentile philosophers. The concluding statement of this chapter details again the source of their teaching:

"These are matters which have, to be sure, the appearance of wisdom in self-made religion and self-abasement and severe treatment of the body, but are of no value against fleshly indulgence" (Col. 2:23). As with the meticulous tradition-keeping Pharisees and scribes of Matthew 15:1—importantly, being addressed by Paul the ex-Pharisee—at the core was a substitution of the Word of God in place of the religious, well-meaning—but if followed to its end—eternally damning word of fallen man. In harsh contrast to the false teachers who had attacked the church at Colossae, Paul had previously praised the Thessalonians for their appropriate reception—and recognition—of the true source of Paul's teaching: "And for this reason we also constantly thank God that when you received from us the word of God's message, you accepted it not as the word of men, but for what it really is, the word of God, which also performs its work in you who believe" (1 Thess. 2:13).

You can include the rabbis in teaching this man-made substitution of fallen man's word in place of or mingled with the pure Word of God, both in biblical times and up through our modern day. Paul wrote post-resurrection, decades removed from Jerusalem, and in the Gentile world. Yet this foundational difference did not ever go away, and many still hold to the teachings of men and equate them with what God teaches, and even worse, they teach others to follow their example. You can read all of Matthew 23 if you want to see some of the most condemning denouncements Jesus ever gave. Two statements will suffice: "But woe to you, scribes and Pharisees, hypocrites, because you shut off the kingdom of heaven from men; for you do not enter in yourselves, nor do you allow those who are entering to go in" (Matt. 23:13), and "Woe to you, scribes and Pharisees, hypocrites, because you travel about on sea and land to make one proselyte; and when he becomes one, you make him twice as much a son of hell as yourselves" (Matt. 23:15).

In the parallel account to Matthew 15, Mark 7:13 gives one additional statement, noting "thus invalidating the word of God by your tradition which you have handed down; and you do *many* things such as that." Jesus could have gone down a long list of man-made traditions that the rabbis and Pharisees held as equal to the inspired Word of God and were taught as binding, authoritative doctrine. For our study at hand, we will limit this to one crucial item of tradition that has been passed on through the centuries by the Jewish sages: *the religious, man-made restriction not ever—under any circumstances—to utter the unspeakable name of Yahweh "the Lord."*

It is universally held and easily seen in Scripture that at least until the destruction of God's Temple in 586 B.C., the Jewish people uttered the name of the Lord—as He fully intended. As we have seen, "people began to call on the name of the Lord" is how Genesis 4 ends. In Exodus 3, when Moses asked God's name, God did not say, "I will not tell you, and even if I did, you are never to utter it again." But by the time of at least the third century B.C., based on a misunderstanding of the Third Commandment not to take the Lord's name in vain, the Hebrew YHWH or Yahweh began being struck through in the text or changed to the word *Adonai,* also translated as "Lord." In the English text you will see this usually addressed by writing in capital letters Lord when Yahweh occurs and the smaller case "Lord" when Adonai is used. To this day, unless someone carefully studies the text and knows what it says, in the public reading of Scripture in both synagogues and churches, there is no way for the listener to discern whether "Lord" or "Lord" is used. The Greek translation *kurios,* because it is Greek, would be no problem to the Hebrew writer or reader to write or say. But this is important because it relates to the name of God. Even our word "Jehovah" is a failed attempt of early Christians to take the four consonants of the Hebrew YHWH with the vowels of Adonai and in essence make it a hybrid word.

For the Hebrew reading of Scripture, *Adonai* was and still is routinely substituted for Yahweh. Modern Jews alleviate this man-made problem by substituting *HaShem* ("the Name") whenever Yahweh occurs in the text. Leviticus 19:12 is an example where "the Name" was considered equivalent to the name of Yahweh: "And you shall not swear falsely by My name, so as to profane the name [*HaShem*] of your God; I am the LORD." If Adonai precedes YHWH in the text, another name for God, *Elohim*, would often be substituted. All of this is a man-made tradition that became taught as God's commandment, and it was considered binding and blasphemous if one ever spoke "the unutterable Name (of the LORD)." While this may sound respectful and may initially seem to be religious wisdom, from about the third century B.C. onward, woe be to the one foolish enough to speak the name that should never be spoken. One rabbi went so far as to write, "Whoever pronounces the Name forfeits his portion in the future life" (Sand. 11.1). And thus it was—and still is—taught. Knowing this background helps to explain why Jesus infuriated the Jews, and it explains their response in John 8:58–59: "Jesus said to them, 'Truly, truly, I say to you, before Abraham was born, I AM.' Therefore they picked up stones to throw at Him; but Jesus hid Himself, and went out of the temple." Jesus had spoken "The Name," and He—and any other offender—would be considered blasphemous and worthy of instantaneous execution. By the way, when Moses originally conveyed the name of the LORD to those whom God had commanded him to in Exodus 6:1–8, they did not pick up stones to stone him; they had no reason to do so.

How burdensome these man-made restraints were and are! How tragically sad for Jewish individuals who were/are taught that instead of using God's revealed name Yahweh, the covenant keeping name of God, they are taught never to utter it. Instead of calling on the name of the LORD in prayer, Yahweh becomes an unknown name for God, unutterable and far-removed from them. Sadly, many Jewish people conclude that if they do not utter "Yahweh," then they must be considered righteous, and have no need for salvation—or a Savior.

And equally worse for national Israel are the far-reaching and tremendously damaging ramifications that not speaking this name entails. For instance, first, under such teaching, they collectively will never enjoy the intended blessing of Numbers 6:24–27:

> The LORD bless you, and keep you;
> The LORD make His face shine on you, and be
>   gracious to you;
> The LORD lift up His countenance on you, and give
> you peace.

And remember the important next verse: "So they shall invoke My name on the sons of Israel, and I then will bless them."

It should be noted that "Yahweh" is used in each verse in the blessing of Numbers 6. God intended this as warmly personal, not the sterile and isolated, "The Name bless you and keep you. The Name make His face shine on you." Also, by not invoking God's name properly, national Israel cannot receive God's blessing (Num. 6:27). It will not be until Zechariah 12:10, when the LORD pours out His Spirit of grace and supplication, and they look on Him whom they have pierced, and mourn for Him as an only Son," that the Jewish nation collectively will be brought again into covenant obedience with Yahweh and become recipient of all that this blessing entails. Sadly, this will occur in the midst of the Tribulation, and much must occur before that takes place—such as the nation collectively receiving the Antichrist before they receive Jesus Christ (Dan. 9:24–27; Matt. 24:15–24).

The second tragedy regarding the Jewish people and the man-made prohibition regarding God's name is that it makes "The Temple of the LORD" take on an impersonal tone by being referred to as

"The First Temple" or "The Second Temple." Whose temple? "We can't say." To this day it takes the eternal focus off of *God's* Temple or The Temple *of the* LORD and makes it very impersonal. Even worse is that many people call it "Solomon's Temple" for the First Temple, and horribly, wretched, wretched "Herod's Temple" for the Second Temple. Read your Scripture cover-to-cover, beloved; I assure you that God never called His own Temple by these man-made designations. How profane, how non-honoring to the true God that "this house that is called by His name" (Jer. 7:11) is routinely called by someone else's name. You will not find this to be the case with any of the pagans in whose honor the temples were built. For instance, "The Temple of Baal," "The Temple of Diana," or "The Temple of Zeus" are names always used for those temples, but sadly, the name "The Temple of the LORD" is almost universally not used. Failure to use this name is of the evil one because it takes the focus away from God and His holy work and from His eternal promises. Satan never wants people to focus on the true God "who has placed His name there forever" (1 Kings 9:3), which, of course, includes even today. One would *never* understand the eternal significance of what has transpired—and will transpire—at this exact God-ordained place in Jerusalem without the proper use of God's name as God intended in His city Jerusalem which He Himself has chosen.

And finally, how utterly tragic for the Jewish people that most of them would not initially accept the Messiah who would come to them in the name of the LORD.

CHAPTER FIVE

THE SON

God gave the tremendous privileges and stipulations in the eternally important Davidic Covenant first revealed in 2 Samuel 7:8–16:

> Now therefore, thus you shall say to My servant David, "Thus says the LORD of hosts, I took you from the pasture, from following the sheep, to be ruler over My people Israel. I have been with you wherever you have gone and have cut off all your enemies from before you; and I will make you a great name, like the names of the great men who are on the earth. I will also appoint a place for My people Israel and will plant them, that they may live in their own place and not be disturbed again, nor will the wicked afflict them any more as formerly, even from the day that I commanded judges to be over My people Israel; and I will give you rest from all your enemies. The LORD also declares to you that the LORD will make a house for you.
>
> "When your days are complete and you lie down with your fathers, I will raise up your descendant after you, who will come forth from you, and I will establish his kingdom. He shall build a house for My name, and I will establish the throne of his kingdom forever.
>
> "I will be a father to him and he will be a son to Me; when he commits iniquity, I will correct him with the rod of

men and the strokes of the sons of men, but My lovingkindness shall not depart from him, as I took it away from Saul, whom I removed from before you.

Your house and your kingdom shall endure before Me forever; your throne shall be established forever."

Because of this eternal covenant that God Himself had made (Ps. 89:1–4), whoever sat on the throne of Israel had to be of David's house and lineage, or else that person would be a usurper. Accordingly, "son of David" was used for the first heir, Solomon (1 Chron. 29:22; 2 Chron. 1:1; Prov. 1:1). It was also used of "The Preacher" in Ecclesiastes 1:1, who most likely was Solomon. Because no Hebrew word exists for grandson or grandfather, the term son of David would demonstrate that he was recognized as the rightful heir or occupant of the throne, especially when used with the definite article, that is "the Son of David." The last son of David to rule on David's throne was Zedekiah, who was captured by Nebuchadnezzar in 586 B.C. when God's Temple was destroyed, and "the times of the Gentiles" had commenced (Luke 21:24). After so long a period of having no Davidic heir to reign on David's throne, Matthew 1:1 takes on a more important emphasis: "The beginning of the genealogy of Jesus Christ, the son of David, the Son of Abraham." Matthew began by noting two eternally important covenants that God had made, but he moved them out of their chronological order; the Abrahamic Covenant was about one thousand years before the Davidic Covenant. So with this emphasis, everything in the Gospel of Matthew, which was originally written for a Jewish audience, supports the Messianic claims of Jesus. Notice, however, that not every "son of David" necessarily sat on David's throne. Joseph is also called "son of David" in Matthew 1:20.

Included in this divine covenant was the close relationship that God and the Davidic Covenant heir would enjoy. Second Samuel 7:14 records that God Himself states, "I will be a father to him, and he will be a son to Me." So in the broadest, most generic meaning possible, whoever sat on David's throne was in a sense "son of God" by adoption—but not by birth—and the sonship began whenever the rightful heir ascended to the throne. That was a high privilege of the Davidic Covenant, but sadly, many of the sons of David who ruled over Israel, and later Judah, had no saving relationship with God who not only had placed them on the throne, but who also desired a Father/son fellowship with them as well.

Since the last day that Zedekiah ruled and was removed from his throne in 586 B.C. (2 Kings 25:1–7), up to our present time, no one has sat on David's throne, making this a period of about 2,600 years. Because of this absence of any rightful ruler to occupy David's throne, several Scripture verses promised One—the Messiah—meaning "the LORD's anointed," such as given in (Ps. 2:2), who would eventually rule and reign over everything, as so found in Psalm 2:1–2:

> Why are the nations in an uproar, and the peoples devising a vain thing?
> The kings of the earth take their stand, and the rulers take counsel together against the LORD and against His anointed.

In this recognized Messianic psalm (by Jews and Gentiles alike) is the claim and the expectation, "I will surely tell of the decree of the LORD: He said to Me, 'You are My Son, today I have begotten You'" (Ps. 2:7). Based on the previous father-son relationship as seen in 2 Samuel 7:14, this verse by itself does not require "Son of God" in a unique sense. Also, technically speaking, the word "Messiah" speaks more of the right to reign and rule—itself not requiring a substitutionary atonement. God referred to His Anointed as "My King" (Ps. 2:6). John 1:41 explains that the words "Messiah" (Hebrew word) and "Christ" (Greek word) were used interchangeably: "He [Andrew] found first his own brother Simon, and said to him, 'We have found the Messiah' (which translated means Christ)."

In another Messianic prophecy, God made specific promises regarding this blessed One who would ultimately come and reign on David's throne:

> For a child will be born to us, a son will be given to us; and the government will rest on His shoulders; and His name will be called Wonderful Counselor, Mighty God, Eternal Father, Prince of Peace. There will be no end to the increase of His government or of peace, on the throne of David and over his kingdom, to establish it and to uphold it with justice and righteousness from then on and forevermore. The zeal of the LORD of hosts will accomplish this (Isa. 9:6–7).

More encouraging about this prophecy is that at the time when Isaiah received this revelation from God, the descendants of David were currently reigning on David's throne (Isa. 1:1). Through His prophet, God spoke of a time in the future when One would come who would eventually reign on David's throne—and rule over the entire world (Ps. 2:7–9). The Jews had good reason to expect this; hundreds of biblical prophecies talk about the King and His Kingdom. Ruler. King. Smite the nations. Worldwide authority and dominion. Israel elevated to the pinnacle of all the nations. Worldwide peace. What a birthright this one must have! What a pedigree! What a promise of a conqueror.

And then, instead, One appeared "who would have no form or majesty that we should look upon Him, nor appearance that we should be attracted to Him, as a man of sorrows, acquainted with grief" (Isa. 53:2–3).

♦ ♦ ♦ ♦ ♦ ♦

The angel Gabriel appears four times in Scripture with each manifestation having one highly significant element in common: special revelation from God concerning who rules the nation of Israel, both bad and good. In Daniel 8, God gave the elderly Daniel a vision regarding the enemies of Israel—including prophecies that ultimately include the Antichrist—culminating with the promised victorious reign of the Messiah. Once the vision ended, God also sent His holy messenger to his beloved prophet to explain the importance of what had just been conveyed:

> And it came about when I, Daniel, had seen the vision, that I sought to understand it; and behold, standing before me was one who looked like a man.
> And I heard the voice of a man between the banks of Ulai, and he called out and said, "Gabriel, give this man an understanding of the vision" (Daniel 8:15–16).

You can read more about this extremely important prophecy from God in Daniel 8. In the next chapter Gabriel again appears to Daniel who is praying for God to fulfill His promises concerning Jerusalem and, even more to the point, God's Temple that had been destroyed. While we do not have time to linger in this eternally important chapter of prophecy, we can at least see Gabriel's highly important role to reveal to God's long-time faithful prophet who believed both God and His Word, as shown in Daniel 9:20–22:

> Now while I [Daniel] was speaking and praying, and confessing my sin and the sin of my people Israel, and presenting my supplication before the LORD my God in behalf of the holy mountain of my God, while I was still speaking in prayer, then the man Gabriel, whom I had seen in the vision previously, came to me in my extreme weariness

about the time of the evening offering. And he gave me instruction and talked with me, and said, "O Daniel, I have now come forth to give you insight with understanding."

Daniel 9:24–27 concludes this enormously important prophecy and explanation with the promise of the seven-year Tribulation, the covenant the Antichrist will make with the nation of Israel to rebuild God's Temple and to restore the sacrifices, as well as the Antichrist's breaking of this covenant at the midpoint of the Tribulation. This "abomination of desolation" (Dan. 9:27) was what Jesus quoted in Matthew 24:15 to explain matters regarding the future destruction of God's Temple, His own personal return, and the end of the age (Matt. 21:1–14). These prophetic gold mines contain so much more, but we must move on with our study at hand. Those who want to study the significance of these verses in more detail can read *The Stone and the Glory*, or *The Stone and the Glory of Israel*, if they have not already done so.

The next time Gabriel appears is approximately five hundred years later in God's Temple as he appeared to an elderly priest named Zacharias. Gabriel brought God's revelation that Zacharias and his wife Elizabeth were to become the parents of the promised forerunner of the Messiah (Isaiah 40:3; Luke 1:11–20). The first two appearances of Gabriel in the Book of Daniel focused primarily on the enemies of Israel who would reign; this third message related the wonderful news of the soon coming birth of the Messiah. However, instead of rejoicing in what God had revealed, Zacharias, the doubting priest, aggravated God's holy messenger as Gabriel stated the importance of his own angelic status and then revealed the consequence of the priest's lack of belief in the Word of God:

> And Zacharias said to the angel, "How shall I know this for certain? For I am an old man, and my wife is advanced in years."

> And the angel answered and said to him, "I am Gabriel, who stands in the presence of God; and I have been sent to speak to you, and to bring you this good news.
>
> "And behold, you shall be silent and unable to speak until the day when these things take place, because you did not believe my words, which shall be fulfilled in their proper time" (Luke 1:18–20).

The final appearance in Scripture of "Gabriel, who stands in the presence of God" occurs to a much more receptive heart to both God and His Word:

> Now in the sixth month the angel Gabriel was sent from God to a city in Galilee, called Nazareth, to a virgin engaged to a man whose name was Joseph, of the descendants of David; and the virgin's name was Mary.
>
> And coming in, he said to her, "Hail, favored one! The Lord is with you."
>
> But she was greatly troubled at this statement, and kept pondering what kind of salutation this might be.
>
> And the angel said to her, "Do not be afraid, Mary; for you have found favor with God.
>
> "And behold, you will conceive in your womb, and bear a son, and you shall name Him Jesus. He will be great, and will be called the Son of the Most High; and the Lord God will give Him the throne of His father David; and He will reign over the house of Jacob forever; and His kingdom will have no end" (Luke 1:26–33).

Mary had questions about how this was possible since nothing like this had ever happened before—or ever would occur again—but this humble lover of God and His Word did not question whether this promised Virgin Birth would actually happen, as Luke 1:34–38 reveals:

> And Mary said to the angel, "How can this be, since I am a virgin?"
>
> And the angel answered and said to her, "The Holy Spirit will come upon you, and the power of the Most High will overshadow you; and for that reason the holy offspring shall be called the Son of God.
>
> "And behold, even your relative Elizabeth has also conceived a son in her old age; and she who was called barren is now in her sixth month. For nothing will be impossible with God."
>
> And Mary said, "Behold, the bondslave of the Lord; be it done to me according to your word." And the angel departed from her.

We should especially note the importance of Luke 1:32 and 1:35. God promised that the Messiah would be called "the son of the Most High," and yet "the Lord God will give Him the throne of His father David," that is, as part of the Davidic Covenant and the human ancestry from which the Messiah would be born—just as Scripture previously mandated in passages such as Isaiah 9:6–7. Just to make sure this was not misinterpreted or taken to mean something that it did not, Gabriel again underscored the importance of the Virgin Birth by declaring "for this reason the holy offspring shall be called the Son of God" (Luke 1:35), the first occurrence of any "holy offspring" since Adam's fall and the resulting contamination for all of his other multitudes of descendants. So that which was previewed in previous prophecies now became specifically and openly declared in private, and would one day be proclaimed around the world; the Messiah would be both the Son of David (human part) and the Son of God (Godhead status).

The Jews of Jesus' time, however, and many Jews to this present time who have not believed that the Messiah has yet come would answer the question, "Whose son is the Messiah?" by saying simply, "The Son of David." Period. They considered, or presently consider, that the Messiah will be elevated and exalted above all humanity, but he will not be divine, and certainly he will not be equal with God the Father. Interestingly, legions of demons in one man (Luke 8:30) referred to Jesus as they knew Him to be: "What do I have to do with you, Jesus, Son of the Most High God?" (Luke 8:28)—not Son of David—echoing back to Gabriel's divine revelation to Mary in Luke 1. The phrase "the Son of David" shows that the rightful heir can trace his lineage back to David—a mandatory requirement for the Messiah—and that he is fully of the tribe of Judah, of the house of David, as Joseph was shown to be in Luke 1:27 and 2:4. But Messiah as the Son of God? Only in the most generic, restricted way that we saw in the Davidic Covenant promise of 2 Samuel 7:14 would this be accepted by any unbelieving Jew.

We encounter the first of many instances in the life of Jesus regarding both His origin and identity with concerns expressed by Nathanael in John 1:43–50:

> The next day He purposed to go into Galilee, and He found Philip. And Jesus said to him, "Follow Me." Now Philip was from Bethsaida, of the city of Andrew and Peter. Philip found Nathanael and said to him, "We have found Him of whom Moses in the Law and also the Prophets wrote—Jesus of Nazareth, the son of Joseph."
>
> Nathanael said to him, "Can any good thing come out of Nazareth?" Philip said to him, "Come and see."
>
> Jesus saw Nathanael coming to Him, and said of him, "Behold, an Israelite indeed, in whom there is no deceit!" Nathanael said to Him, "How do You know me?" Jesus

answered and said to him, "Before Philip called you, when you were under the fig tree, I saw you."

Nathanael answered Him, "Rabbi, You are the Son of God; You are the King of Israel."

Jesus answered and said to him, "Because I said to you that I saw you under the fig tree, do you believe? You will see greater things than these."

Nathaniel proclaimed to Jesus in John 1:49: "Rabbi, *You* are the Son of God; *You* are the King of Israel," with both times "You" being emphatic in the Greek text. Notice that he said "Son of God"—not "Son of David." Philip did not rebuke Nathanael for what he said—nor did Jesus. Furthermore, Jesus did not correct Nathanael for his erroneous statement; by lack of Jesus' action, He accepted what was said in reference to Him. This encounter was in some of the earliest parts of Jesus' ministry. He would have much, much more to disclose about who He is and what He had come to do. Interestingly, either Nathanael was *extremely* spiritually astute (because, after all, what he spoke was one hundred per cent accurate), or he used the title "son of God" in the broadest, most generic sense as he possibly could.

Just one little side note: several times at the campuses where I have taught I have seen students studying outside (especially in Spring or Fall). Many times I would say, "I saw you studying under the tree." Not one time has anyone ever said to me after I told him or her this, "Rabbi, you are the Son of God; You are the King of Israel." Perhaps because of the limitations in that I am both a Gentile and am sinful, it would suffice that I do not qualify. But let's put it this way: something more happened in the account of Nathanael and Jesus. We do not know exactly what occurred because the Bible does not tell us. Jesus could have quoted the verses Nathanael was reading or could have given indication that He knew what Nathanael had either said or prayed—or both. But it was enough for Nathaniel to respond in reflexive exuberance, "Rabbi, *You* are the Son of God; *You* are the King of Israel." This would be far from the last time that someone said something regarding the identity of Jesus.

When you read through the Gospels you will see that Jesus is addressed from time to time as "Son of David." There is nothing wrong with saying this: He was and is indeed the Son of David, and as we have seen, this is a designation for the Messiah. For instance, two blind men called out "Have mercy on us, Son of David!" (Matt. 9:27)—not Son of God—which was another way of saying, "We recognize you to be the Messiah sent by God." Because of all the miracles that Jesus performed, plus the added verification He had offered, the core question stood—and still stands—before the Jewish people: "And all multitudes were amazed, and began to say, 'This man cannot be the Son of David, can he?'" (Matt. 12:23)—not Son of God at this point. Relatively soon after that, a Gentile Canaanite woman pleaded "Have mercy on me, O Lord, Son of David; my daughter is demon possessed" (Matt. 15:22). None of these statements are incorrect; none received rebuke from Jesus that they should not be said. Nothing is wrong with what they said; it was merely incomplete without the rest of the story that God was about to fill in.

◆ ◆ ◆ ◆ ◆ ◆ ◆

Matthew 12 is a pivotal chapter in the Gospel of Matthew because major changes take place. After all the affirmation that Jesus had shown, and because His enemies the religious leaders could not deny the miracles that He performed, they denied the source of the miracles: "This man casts out demons by Beelzebul the ruler of the demons" (Matt. 12:24), which is another way of saying that Jesus cast out demons by the power and authority of Satan—not of God. It is in this context that "the unpardonable sin" occurs (Matt. 12:30–32), which summed up briefly meant that the nation of Israel, through her religious leaders, initially rejected Jesus as Messiah. He was—and still remains—King, and the Kingdom most assuredly will come where He will reign on David's throne, but that was not His designated time.

We see the consequences of God's Messiah being rejected in Matthew 13 when Jesus began teaching the people by using parables. Previously, the message had been the same topic preached by John the Baptist (Matt. 3:1–2) and later by Jesus (Matt. 4:17): "Repent! For the kingdom of heaven/God is at hand." When the Twelve were sent out, Jesus limited them to one topic: "The kingdom of heaven is at hand" (Matt. 10:5–7). After Matthew 12, the kingdom was no longer at hand. In Matthew 13, the King and the Kingdom would come at the end of the age (Matt. 13:36–43). God was still in control, and He would fulfill even the smallest part of His promises, but tragically for the nation of Israel, they did not realize the time of God's initial visitation by sending the Messiah to them (Luke 19:44). Some believed; most did not.

Then in Matthew 16, which took place after the national rejection of the Messiah, Jesus had much to teach His disciples. In northern Galilee, at Caesarea Philippi, Jesus broached the subject by asking in Matthew 16:13, "Who do people say the Son of Man is?" The disciples replied, "Some say John the Baptist; and others, Elijah; but still others, Jeremiah, or one of the prophets" (Matt. 16:14). It is noteworthy that the answer did not include "Son of Beelzebul" or "Son of Satan," as the religious leaders had previously called Him in Matthew 12. More to the point, Jesus further raised a question that ultimately *all individuals* must answer, with the outcome of their eternity based on how they respond to Him, "He said to them, 'But who do you say that I am?'" (Matt. 16:15). Peter responded by answering, "You are the Christ/Messiah, the Son of the living God" (Matt. 16:16)—in this case, not the Son of David. The Greek text contains four definite articles giving in its literal translation a most specific designation: "You are *the* Messiah/Christ (not a Messiah), *the*

Son of *the* God *the* living One." Notice, too, that even though "the Unpardonable Sin" of the nation of Israel by temporarily rejecting Jesus as Messiah in Matthew 12 had already transpired, their rejection had absolutely nothing to do with who Jesus is, what He would do, and what He will do in the future, including ultimately reigning over all the world and as King and having His capital in Jerusalem. We see this in the present tense form of the verb that Peter employed: "You *are* the Messiah/Christ," not "You *were* the Messiah, but the nation through its religious leaders rejected You forever."

Although many who are saved and are part of the Body of Christ may think that Peter's statement was not substantial, God knew it was. In fact, the Father made sure that Peter got every scintilla of the answer correct, as Jesus explained in Matthew 16:17, "And Jesus answered and said to him, 'Blessed are you, Simon Barjona, because flesh and blood did not reveal this to you, but My Father who is in heaven.'" Peter's statement was not of man-made philosophy, Jewish wisdom, or observant deduction. God the Father gave Peter direct divine revelation about God the Son, as He would give to all of His prophets and to the apostles who would come later (2 Pet. 1:20–21; 1 Thess. 2:13). God used Peter to convey divine revelation about the person and the work of Jesus the Son of David, the Son of Abraham (Matt. 1:1). After years of training His chosen Twelve (Matt. 10:1–2), whom Jesus previously prohibited from going to the Gentiles, but rather at that time only to the lost sheep of the house Israel proclaiming, "The Kingdom of heaven is at hand" (Matt. 10: 5–7), the Apostles from this time onward received more and more teaching by Jesus about exactly Who the King is. The Kingdom of Heaven/God is of utmost importance, being the content of most of the subject matter that Jesus used as He taught the eleven after His resurrection but before His Ascension:

The first account I composed, Theophilus, about all that Jesus began to do and teach, until the day when He was taken up, after He had by the Holy Spirit given orders to the apostles whom He had chosen. To these He also presented Himself alive, after His suffering, by many convincing proofs, appearing to them over a period of forty days, and speaking of the things concerning the kingdom of God" (Acts 1:1–3).

Matthew 16:13–17:13 is one of *the* most important sections in the entire Bible. In fact, much of how these passages are interpreted (or misinterpreted) will affect just about every other passage of Scripture before these verses and afterwards—all the way up to the end of the Book of Revelation. Notice "the spiritual bombshells" that Jesus gave in this section; mark as well that this portion of Scripture at this time was done in private by Jesus as He began to prepare His apostles for what lay ahead. They would tell this message many, many times for the rest of their lives, but this was the timing for private training by "The Messiah/Christ, the Son of the God, the living One." We cannot linger at each one of these foundational truths, but at least we can note them. In continuation of Jesus' answer to Peter and the others, He explained, "I also say to you that you are Peter, and upon this rock I will build My church; and the gates of Hades will not overpower it. I will give you the keys of the kingdom of heaven; and whatever you bind on earth shall have been bound in heaven, and whatever you loose on earth shall have been loosed in heaven" (Matt. 16:18–19). For the first time in the entire Bible the word "church" is used, and of utmost importance, Jesus used a future tense verb: "I will build My church." The original hearers of Jesus' use of the future tense never got over the fact that they expected the King and the Kingdom to arrive immediately—even until Jesus was betrayed in the Garden (Luke 19:11). Jesus knew they could not comprehend this, but He would patiently teach them, as they were able to receive, especially after His resurrection. In Matthew 16:20 Jesus restricted what He would one day commission them to do on a worldwide basis: "Then He warned the disciples that they should tell no one that He was the Christ/Messiah." They would eventually tell, but Jesus had much more to teach them.

Matthew 16 contains another earth-shattering divine revelation: "From that time Jesus began to show His disciples that He must go to Jerusalem and suffer many things from the elders and chief priests and scribes, and be killed, and be raised up on the third day" (Matt. 16:21). Previously, Jesus had alluded to His death; now He began to teach them, in this first of many times, that He must go to Jerusalem, be killed by the religious leaders, but be raised on the third day. This account includes Peter's first attempt to keep Jesus from going to the cross, and in diametrical opposites regarding the true source of God in Matthew 16:17, this time the source was Satan (Matt. 16:22–23). This section reveals for the first time the cost of true discipleship: "Then Jesus said to His disciples, 'If anyone wishes to come after Me, he must deny himself, and take up his cross and follow Me. For whoever wishes to save his life will lose it; but whoever loses his life for My sake will find it'" (Matt. 16:24–25). This teaching was new and was hard to receive by those who had already proclaimed the Kingdom was at hand, but who were still expecting the advent of the King and His Kingdom. Nonetheless, Jesus spoke the truth. Matthew 16 ends with another tremendously important statement by Jesus, as for the first time in all of His teaching He taught on the Glory of God, and—of utmost importance—He applied this glory to Himself and to His Second Advent: "Truly I say to you, there are some of those who are standing here who will not taste death until they see the Son of Man coming in His kingdom" (Matt. 16:28). The Transfiguration that followed (Matt. 17:1–8) was a preview of what the

King and the Kingdom will look like when He returns to reign in glory (2 Pet. 1:16–18).

As the King headed to Jerusalem, He was hailed by two blind men in Matthew 20:30–31, and they cried out "Lord, have mercy on us, Son of David!"—not Son of God. Not that this was wrong, as they called out to Him as the promised Messiah, but their understanding was not nearly as mature as the teaching that Jesus had given in private to the Twelve. Yet a few days before His own death, one very close disciple of Jesus did understand His ultimate identity:

> So when Jesus came, He found that he [Lazarus] had already been in the tomb four days. Now Bethany was near Jerusalem, about two miles off; and many of the Jews had come to Martha and Mary, to console them concerning their brother. Martha therefore, when she heard that Jesus was coming, went to meet Him; but Mary still sat in the house.
>
> Martha therefore said to Jesus, "Lord, if You had been here, my brother would not have died. Even now I know that whatever You ask of God, God will give You."
>
> Jesus said to her, "Your brother shall rise again."
>
> Martha said to Him, "I know that he will rise again in the resurrection on the last day" (John 11:17–24).

Note the core question contained in the following sentence that Jesus asked Martha: "I am the resurrection and the life; he who believes in Me shall live even if he dies, and everyone who lives and believes in Me shall never die. Do you believe this?" (John 11:25–26).

Note the core answer that Martha gave in response to what Jesus had asked her: "She said to Him, 'Yes, Lord; I have believed that You are the Christ, the Son of God, even He who comes into the world'"

(John 11:27)—not the Son of David, spoken by a lover of God's Word, and appropriately at this point, spoken to Him in private.

Both titles for Messiah are important and appropriate for the truth to be told. However, the title Son of God used for the Messiah was then and remains now a stumbling block to many of the Jewish people (and others). Saul the Pharisee before he was saved had people tortured and killed who would call Jesus the Messiah Son of God. Messiah the Son of David, the Jews did and still do expect; the Messiah the Son of God—utter blasphemy worthy of death. How appropriate that immediately after his salvation in Acts 9:19–20, Paul's testimony changed: "Now for several days he was with the disciples who were at Damascus, and immediately he began to proclaim Jesus in the synagogues, saying, 'He is the Son of God'"—not the Son of David. Paul was a quick learner, indeed, as Acts 9:21–22 explains the amazement of those who listened and the present ministry of Saul the Christian who would eventually become Paul the Apostle: "All those hearing him continued to be amazed, and were saying, 'Is this not he who in Jerusalem destroyed those who called on this name, and who had come here for the purpose of bringing them bound before the chief priests?' But Saul kept increasing in strength and confounding the Jews who lived at Damascus by proving that this Jesus is the Christ/Messiah."

So when Jesus rode into Jerusalem in what many erroneously call "the Triumphal Entry," He received Messianic acclamation, all based on His being the Son of David:

> And most of the multitude spread their garments in the road, and others were cutting branches from the trees, and spreading them in the road. And the multitudes going before Him, and those who followed after were crying out, saying, "Hosanna to the Son of David; blessed is He who comes in the name of the Lord; Hosanna in the highest!" And when He had entered Jerusalem, all the city was

stirred, saying, "Who is this?" And the multitudes were saying, "This is the prophet Jesus, from Nazareth in Galilee" (Matt. 21:8–11).

Notice how limited the nation's understanding about Jesus was at this time. They knew He was special; many knew He was sent from God, but He would very soon demonstrate that He was much, much more than "the prophet Jesus, from Nazareth in Galilee" by showing in God's own Word that this particular Son of David also uniquely came in the name of the LORD.

◆ ◆ ◆ ◆ ◆ ◆ ◆

Matthew 21–22 contains events of two strategic days of revealing that the final countdown to Calvary had begun in earnest. As with Matthew 16, there are so many goldmines here that we cannot linger in, but at least some of these can be marked for later study. After arriving in Jerusalem amidst the tumultuous proclamation of the massive multitudes assembled, Jesus cleansed His own Temple (Matt. 21:12–13). He healed the blind and the lame in His newly purified Temple (Matt. 21:14). A section of the religious authorities showed their incensed response: "But when the chief priests and the scribes saw the wonderful things that He had done, and the children who were shouting in the temple, Hosanna to the Son of David [not Son of God], they became indignant" (Matt. 21:15).

The authority of Jesus was challenged (Matt. 21:23–27), which Jesus turned back on His questioners by asking whether the source of authority for John the Baptist was from God or man? He used their utter lack of an answer to give the Parable of the Two Sons (Matt. 21:28–32) and the Parable of the Landowner (Matt. 21:33–46). Of utmost importance was Jesus' use of "the Stone Prophecies" in relation to the Messiah who stood before them. You can read more about these in *The Stone and the Glory* in the chapters entitled "The Lesson" Part 1 and Part 2. Divine Messianic prophecies were being fulfilled before their eyes, but it would certainly not be the last of such prophecies:

> Jesus said to them, "Did you never read in the Scriptures,
> 'THE STONE WHICH THE BUILDERS REJECTED,
> THIS BECAME THE CHIEF CORNER STONE;
> THIS CAME ABOUT FROM THE LORD,
> AND IT IS MARVELOUS IN OUR EYES'?
> "Therefore I say to you, the kingdom of God will be taken away from you, and be given to a nation producing the fruit of it. And he who falls on this stone will be broken to pieces; but on whomever it falls, it will scatter him like dust."
> And when the chief priests and the Pharisees heard His parables, they understood that He was speaking about them (Matt. 21:42–45).

Among other things, Matthew 22 records the trick questions asked by hostile religious foes, one in reference to paying taxes to Caesar (Matt. 22:15–22), and the other in an attempt by the wicked Sadducees, "who say there is no resurrection," attempting to cause Him to stumble over the doctrine of the resurrection (Matt. 22:23–32). None of them were seeking truth from Him; they were seeking to publicly ridicule this One whom they deemed a liar and an imposter. However, He was neither, and He spoke the truth with the result being, "when the multitudes heard this, they were astonished at His teaching" (Matt. 22:32).

Still in this context, Jesus turned to the Pharisees as He took the initiative to confront them. Interestingly, once Jesus had rebuked the Sadducees, He did not include them in this question in Matthew

22:41–42: "Now while the Pharisees were gathered together, Jesus asked them a question: 'What do you think about the Christ/Messiah, whose son is He?' They said to Him, 'The son of David.'" The Pharisees were among the religious elite of their day; they were the Ph.D.'s in Jewish theology. Yet the question that Jesus asked was such that most kindergarten-age Jewish children could have answered. It would be similar to gathering the collective history departments of the most elite universities in America and then ask them, "Who was the first president of the United States?"

"What do you think about the Christ/Messiah, whose son is He?"

"David's son, of course! Is this the best that you have to ask us?" How childishly simple and insulting this question was to them.

Note how Jesus then countered in Matthew 22:43–45:

> He said to them, "Then how does David in the Spirit call Him 'Lord,' saying, 'The LORD said to my Lord, sit at My right hand, until I put your enemies beneath Your feet'"?
>
> "If David then calls Him 'Lord,' how is He his son?"

Note the effect that this had on both the original questioners and all others present: "No one was able to answer Him a word, nor did anyone dare from that day on to ask Him another question" (Matt. 22:46). So why this astonishment? Why this massive, amazing response of the people to this simple question that Jesus asked?

Simply put, the Incarnate Word of God quoted the written Word of God, and with one simple question based on one verse from Psalm 110:1, Jesus dismantled their entire theology. The Pharisees had many problems, especially as they elevated their traditions as being equal to—or even above—God's Word, but at least this group (for the most part) believed the Scriptures. Consequently, you will find in the Book of Acts instances where Pharisees were eventually saved (Acts 15:5), and as we saw, this would include the Apostle Paul

(Phil. 3:4–5). But in the Matthew 22 account they stood that day as hostile adversaries. So Jesus took their answer regarding the Messiah as being David's son because *never* under any circumstances would they have answered that the Messiah was the Son of God.

Jesus took one Scripture passage from the Holy Word that they claimed to believe and asked them to answer the theological significance of David's Psalm 110:1: "The LORD said to my Lord." In the Hebrew it is "Yahweh said to Adonai." Most of the original audience would have substituted "*HaShem*" "the Name" for Yahweh, or inserted Adonai in place of Yahweh. And yet here, plainly seen in Scripture, is that one cannot substitute Adonai in place of Yahweh because then the verse would make no sense whatsoever: "Adonai said to Adonai, sit at My right hand until I make your enemies a footstool for your feet?" Adonai talks to Himself? But this cannot be right because someone is supposed to sit at His right hand? But who possibly qualifies to sit at the right hand of Yahweh, which would mean equal authority with and total acceptance by Yahweh?

But as unanswerable as these questions were—and remain and will not go away—for those who attempt to limit God, equally unanswerable observations that lead to staggering questions cascade in childlike simplicity over the waterfall of the holy logic of God. To begin with, and in answer to Jesus' question regarding whose son is the Messiah, David addresses him as "My Lord,"—not "My son." Not only that, this One is David's Lord *before* He would ever be born, which makes Him pre-eternal. David used no future tense. He did not say, "Yahweh will say to my son who will one day be born and outrank me and be my Lord." No one else in the history of the world was pre-eternal except this One, and if you believe God's Word you *must* identify who this One is of whom David prophesied, but God does not give people many options as to who qualifies. Anyone who does not properly identify to Whom Psalm 110:1 refers, stands condemned in their own disbelief as much as the original questioners of

Jesus in Matthew 22. God forces people to answer who Jesus is. And as some of you, no doubt, have already reasoned, if He is pre-eternal, then He is demonstrating attributes of God. Also, instead of being rebuked for what some would consider blasphemy, God elevates the One to a sacred position of honored status at His very right hand.

One more crucially important related item remains, but this does not exhaust their usage or importance. In Matthew 26:63–66, after false witnesses testified against Jesus at His hurried and illegal nighttime trial, the following exchange took place:

> But Jesus kept silent. And the high priest said to Him, "I adjure You by the living God, that You tell us whether You are the Christ, the Son of God."
>
> Jesus said to him, "You have said it yourself; nevertheless I tell you, hereafter you shall see the Son of Man sitting at the right hand of Power, and coming on the clouds of heaven."
>
> Then the high priest tore his robes, saying, "He has blasphemed! What further need do we have of witnesses? Behold, you have now heard the blasphemy; what do you think?" They answered and said, "He is deserving of death!"

Note again what they asked and how Jesus responded: "Are You the Messiah/Christ, the Son of God"—not the Son of David. Being only days after the events of Matthew 22, they knew exactly what they were asking. Considering oneself to be the Son of David was not a capital crime; considering yourself uniquely the Son of God was. Notice also that "I adjure you by the Living God" is identical to Peter's answer in Matthew 16:16 "You are the Christ, the Son of the Living God." But these men had no search for truth; they did not remotely believe. Jesus had no legal reason to respond but chose to by once more referring to the teaching of Psalm 110:1 "sitting at the right hand of Power," and "coming in the clouds of the sky" being taken directly from the Messianic prophecy of Daniel 7:13–14:

> "I kept looking in the night visions, and behold, with the clouds of heaven One like a Son of Man was coming, and He came up to the Ancient of Days and was presented before Him. And to Him was given dominion, glory and a kingdom, that all the peoples, nations, and men of every language might serve Him. His dominion is an everlasting dominion which will not pass away; and His kingdom is one which will not be destroyed.

Son of David—the human part. Son of God—the divine part. Both parts are uniquely true—and divinely required—for this blessed One who came—and is still yet to come again—in the name of the Lord.

CHAPTER SIX

THE COMPANION

Luke 9 was a turning point in the life of Jesus. By the time the events of this chapter unfold, the nation of Israel, through her religious leaders, have rejected—temporarily—Jesus as the Messiah sent by God Himself. In spite of all the manifold ways that the Holy Spirit bore witness and substantiated His Messianic claims, the enemies of the Word claimed rather that He did these miracles only by "the power of Beelzebub" (Matt. 12:22–24), that is, by the power of Satan. Thus they committed "blasphemy against the Holy Spirit" (Matt. 12:32), to which Mark 3:29 adds such ones "never have forgiveness, but are guilty of an eternal sin." Indeed they were guilty, such was the nature of this horrendous attributing of God's work to be that of Satan's power and authority. Jesus was and is still King, and His promised Kingdom was most assuredly going to arrive (Ps. 2; Dan. 7:13–14)— but not now. Later in Acts 2:22–24 we find that this was no surprise to the Godhead:

> "Men of Israel, listen to these words: Jesus the Nazarene, a man attested to you by God with miracles and wonders and signs which God performed through Him in your midst, just as you yourselves know—this Man, delivered over by the predetermined plan and foreknowledge of God, you nailed to a cross by the hands of godless men and put Him to death. But God raised Him

up again, putting an end to the agony of death, since it was impossible for Him to be held in its power."

Later in the book of Acts we see that many who had initially rejected Him as Savior ultimately received both Him and salvation, but in "the predetermined plan and foreknowledge of God" (Acts 2:23), this national rejection was not unexpected. Salvation came on an individual basis—not at this point nationally—as the fulness of the promised Kingdom awaited the Second Advent of the King who will by no means be rejected the second time.

The Twelve minus Judas never completely understood this foundational doctrine until after the death, burial, and resurrection of the Messiah—and after Jesus "opened their minds to understand the Scriptures" (Luke 24:45). Just a few days before the Lamb of God was to take away the sins of the world (John 1:29) and give His life as ransom for many (Mark 10:45), Luke 19:11 reveals the mindset of the Twelve and the multitudes: "And while they were listening to these things, He went on to tell them a parable, because they were near to Jerusalem, and they supposed that the kingdom of God was going to appear *immediately*." How utterly shocking then to them would be the tumultuous events that unfolded that week. They were expecting Him to reign; He was entering the city to die, and at this time none of the Twelve could begin to even mentally grasp that.

About a year earlier, Jesus began preparing His disciples for His impending death in Luke 9:18–27. The parallel accounts in Matthew 16:13–30 and Mark 8:27–30 give a composite of what the rejected Messiah taught His Apostles. In these chapters is the question of "Who do the multitudes say that I am?" followed by the answer "You are the Christ the Son of the Living God." You can go back and read all three chapters, but for our study at hand we will stay in Luke's account. Luke 9:22 was the first time Jesus openly spoke of His death (Luke 9:22), as well as the cost of true discipleship (Luke 9:23). Luke

9:23–27 contains earth-shattering divine revelation, although many students of the Word do not note it, because as we saw in the previous chapter, this was the first time that Jesus ever taught about the Glory of God. Roughly speaking, the Bible contains about one thousand references to the Glory of God, and now Jesus taught about it and tied it in with His Second Coming—not His first—and thus took every reference to the Glory of God and associated Himself with these eternally rich verses.

The Transfiguration followed eight days later (Luke 9:28–36) where God gave three witnesses a preview of what the coming King and Kingdom would look like. But before that transpired, Moses and Elijah appeared and "were speaking of His departure which He was about to accomplish in Jerusalem" (Luke 9:31). Not only did the chosen witnesses hear the audible voice of God and see in this vision the visible presence of Moses and Elijah, but they also witnessed the pinnacle of the event described with the succinct statement, "but when they were fully awake, they saw His glory" (Luke 9:32). No living human beings had ever seen such a special manifestation of God's glory, let alone on the face of the Messiah; but these three had, and they came down the mountain changed forever.

Luke 9:44–45 gives an explanation of not only what was going to happen, but also the mindset of the Twelve: "'Let these words sink into your ears; for the Son of Man is going to be delivered into the hands of men.' But they did not understand this statement, and it was concealed from them so that they might not perceive it; and they were afraid to ask Him about this statement." Often we who live this side of the Cross and have the further revelation from God wonder why they could not believe the words of Jesus. Here is the answer: God concealed it from them that they might not perceive. This is important because it was not only on that day that they could not perceive what Jesus was about to accomplish, but all through the final year of Jesus' life, including from His lowly entry into Jerusalem to His arrest in Gethsemane, His apostles were still expecting Him to reign—not to die. This also helps to explain Peter's actions on the night that Judas betrayed Jesus. And the truth being told, even without God concealing these deep spiritual truths from us, if we had been at the Transfiguration, we likewise would have wondered how *anyone* could possibly have the power to kill this One who had shone brighter than the sun.

On the heels of these saddening events preceding Jesus' death, Luke 9:46 records a stinging rebuke every time I and many others read it: "And an argument arose among them as to which of them might be the greatest." Fallen sinful men in the presence of the Holy One of God debated in relation to themselves as to who was the greatest—and did so in the presence of the One who exceeded all collective fallen humanity. Peter, James, and John had witnessed the transfigurational glory, but they were not permitted to tell anyone else what they saw. It reasons that they listened at this point in their spiritual lives in a rather smugly condescending manner because they knew that whatever those who had not witnessed the Transfiguration brought up as evidence of what they did or why they were the greatest, *nothing else* was remotely in the universe of what God permitted Peter, James and John to behold.

With this background Luke 9:51 becomes monumental in our study: "And it came about, when the days were approaching for His ascension, that He resolutely set His face to go to Jerusalem." Luke 9:52–53 adds the second reference to His face in this passage: "and He sent messengers on ahead of Him. And they went, and entered a village of the Samaritans, to make arrangements for Him. And they did not receive Him, because He was journeying with His face toward Jerusalem," or stated literally from the Greek text, "His face was proceeding toward Jerusalem." How Jesus manifested this resolute determination, we do not know. Yet it was evident to the Samaritans (and most likely to others) that He had set His face. He did so because, first, He had previously announced His death and knew that the Cup that Father had for Him awaited, and second, no doubt because of the intensified satanic opposition against His arrival in Jerusalem. With the unfathomable severity of what He was about to endure, anything less than "a set face" would not be strong enough to endure.

But beyond these two facts remains another important one: biblical prophecies *require* that whoever the Messiah is, this One at some point in His life must set His face. The third of what is called the four "Servant Songs" of Isaiah (Isa. 50:4–11) contains this description of the promised Messiah and what awaited him:

> The Lord GOD has given Me the tongue of disciples, that I may know how to sustain the weary one with a word. He awakens Me morning by morning, He awakens My ear to listen as a disciple. The Lord GOD has opened My ear; and I was not disobedient, nor did I turn back. I gave My back to those who strike Me, and My cheeks to those who pluck out the beard; I did not cover My face [*paneh*] from humiliation and spitting. For the Lord GOD helps Me, therefore, I am not disgraced; therefore, I have set My face [*paneh*] like flint, and I know that I shall not be ashamed (Isa. 50:4–7).

Twice in this passage the word "face" is used. Note the personal aspect of what the Messiah has to do: "I have set My face like flint." In describing the ongoing refusal of the disobedient people to follow God, Yahweh revealed a similar term in regard to the utter hardness of the hearts of the Jews: "But they refused to pay attention, and turned a stubborn shoulder and stopped their ears from hearing. *And they made their hearts like flint* so that they could not hear the law and the words which the LORD of hosts had sent by His Spirit through the former prophets; therefore great wrath came from the LORD of hosts" (Zech. 7:11–12). For the obedient and submissive Jesus, it was an entirely different matter; His heart was tender and He was walking with God—but He still had to set His face like flint. No one set it for Him; no one could. This unique Son of God had resolutely set His face like flint to go to Jerusalem to accomplish what was so desperately needed, beginning in Luke 9:51 and ending within a year, to meet His fate that had awaited Him before the foundation of the world (1 Pet. 1:20).

♦ ♦ ♦ ♦ ♦ ♦

The first part of Mark 10:32 offers a glimpse into how arduous the final trip to Jerusalem was for Jesus as they were approaching Jericho and would soon begin the steep ascent from there to Jerusalem and all that awaited Him: "And they were on the road, going up to Jerusalem, and Jesus was walking on ahead of them; and they were amazed, and those who followed were fearful." Striking in this portion of Scripture is that Jesus—the one who had resolutely set His face like flint—walked ahead of them—alone. The solitary walk of Jesus evoked both amazement and fear in the people. Some of the more liberal minded scholars conclude that this verse was thrown into the text and was not authentic because we have no base of comparison with anyone having been amazed that someone walked ahead of the crowd. The critics of God's Word deduce that after hundreds of thousands, if not millions, of trips, why for some reason should this particular journey be different from all others to the degree that the multitudes would marvel. Those who do not believe and receive the Word of God rightly conclude that Jesus' solitary walk and the response of the people is utter nonsense; those who love God and His Word have a glimpse into how arduous the journey was for our Savior long before Gethsemane and His arrest.

God does not reveal what made the people respond in fearful amazement as Jesus walked alone ahead of them. It reasons that some sort of physical manifestations by Jesus accompanied His walk, with the underlying basis being the spiritual battle raging against Him to keep Him from going to Jerusalem. Jesus may have walked with the effort of someone walking against a hurricane wind, yet with no hurricane present. Not one of those present would have been affected the same way He was because no one else had to set his face like flint to go to Jerusalem—no one else was remotely qualified. No one understood; no one could offer comfort; no one could extend mercy to Him: He walked alone.

And then, in the midst of this spiritual onslaught, the most unexpected events would happen: Jesus would stop what He was doing and talk to people (especially the Twelve) and then no doubt again set His face like flint to go to Jerusalem, walking ahead of the people so that they were amazed. Mark 10:32b–34 shows Jesus stopping for such an encounter: "And again He took the twelve aside and began to tell them what was going to happen to Him, saying, 'Behold, we are going up to Jerusalem, and the Son of Man will be delivered to the chief priests and the scribes; and they will condemn Him to death, and will deliver Him to the Gentiles. And they will mock Him and spit upon Him, and scourge Him, and kill Him, and three days later He will rise again." Luke 18:34 explains again why the Twelve did not understand this: "But the disciples understood none of these things, and the meaning of this statement was hidden from them, and they did not comprehend the things that were said."

Matthew, Mark and Luke all record one special encounter where Jesus stopped on His weary walk to Jerusalem to temporarily "unset His face like flint" so He could extend an act of mercy. Matthew 20:29–34 tells of two blind men; Luke 18:35–43 tells of one. Mark's gospel tells only of one also and even gives his name, which was rare for Mark to do in his Gospel, so we would do well to follow his account:

> And they came to Jericho. And as He was going out from Jericho with His disciples and a great multitude, a blind beggar named Bartimaeus, the son of Timaeus, was sitting by the road. And when he heard that it was Jesus the Nazarene, he began to cry out and say, "Jesus, Son of David [not Son of God], have mercy on me!"
> And many were sternly telling him to be quiet, but he kept crying out all the more, "Son of David, have mercy on me!" (Mark 10:46–48).

Bartimaeus addressed Jesus by His Messianic title—the Son of David—something the religious leaders had long before rejected. A kingdom subject called out to the King, but the King was under no obligation whatsoever to stop and converse with Him. And yet Jesus did just that: "And Jesus stopped and said, 'Call him here.' And they called the blind man, saying to him, 'Take courage, arise! He is calling for you.' And casting aside his cloak, he jumped up, and came to Jesus" (Mark 10:49–50).

When Jesus asked, "What do you want Me to do for you?" the blind man said to Him, "Rabboni, I want to regain my sight!" (Mark 10:51). The fact that Bartimaeus wanted to regain his sight showed that he had not been born blind; for some period of time he had been able to see. Then either by disease or an accident, he had become blind at some undisclosed time in his life. Matthew 20:34 adds a detail as to why Jesus did what He did: "And moved with compassion, Jesus touched their eyes." What a sublime act of compassionate grace by this One who so ardently had set His face like flint to go to Jerusalem, and no doubt He could have received compassion Himself if there had been anyone who could have given it.

Mark 10:52 concludes, "And Jesus said to him, 'Go your way; your faith has made you well.' And immediately he regained his sight and began following Him on the road." So the first thing that Bartimaeus would have seen with his newly healed eyes was the face moved with compassion of the One who had healed him. He would also watch as unexpectedly this compassionate face would change again as He set it like flint to go to Jerusalem. Bartimaeus would not have known about all that was involved in this final trip to Jerusalem for Jesus. He had been encamped in Jericho waiting for the arrival of the Son of David about whom he had probably heard many accounts of other healings that Jesus had performed. In a very real and personal way, Jesus had graciously bestowed on Bartimaeus each of the six items contained in Numbers 6:24–26: the LORD did indeed bless and keep him; the LORD did indeed make His compassionate face to shine upon him and was gracious to him; the LORD did indeed stop and lift up His own countenance on him and gave him peace. Bartimaeus not only received his sight; he received his Savior.

Jesus instructed this one: "Go your way." The text of this miraculous grace gift given by Jesus ends with this account, in the last part of Mark 10:52: "And immediately he [Bartimaeus] regained his sight and began following Him on the road." So in a very real sense, when Jesus said "Go your way," "Your way is now my way." Bartimaeus did not return home; he did not try to find a business endeavor that had eluded him during his prolonged period of blindness. Both Jesus and Bartimaeus gained a companion that day; the companion of one became the companion of the other. Bartimaeus received his sight to see the trip from Jericho to Jerusalem; he saw the masses hail his new companion as the Son of David, as he himself had done earlier in Jericho and had enjoyed being a part of the masses singing the Messianic praises of Psalm 118:26 in Matthew 21:9, "Hosanna to the Son of David; blessed is He who comes in the name of the LORD. Hosanna in the highest." Since "His way is my way," from the moment he received his sight, he would have seen Jesus cleanse the Temple and most likely would have heard Him teaching there. For the first time in years, Bartimaeus had the high privilege of seeing the elements of Passover, when previously he had only smelled them in the intensified manner unique to the blind.

The "Go your way" command followed by the response of Bartimaeus to begin following Him on the road (Mark 10:52) would have led Jesus and His new disciple ultimately to Calvary. If Bartimaeus had been there, and in all likelihood he would have been—having nowhere else to go plus no other interest—he would have been able to read the placard on the cross, "This is Jesus of Nazareth, the King of the Jews." He would eventually have seen his companion's face marred more than that of any other man's (Isa. 52:14). He would have received his sight to see the unexpected and unexplained three-hour darkness over the land. While the newly blind would grovel in fear—if they moved at all—this one so use to maneuvering in environs of darkness would not. While others may flee in terror, he had no reason to do so; darkness was not a stranger to him. Besides, while he did not understand what was transpiring or why it was, he realized that his freshly remade eyes had not lost their capacity to see; the darkness associated with the last three hours of Jesus' crucifixion resided outside of him, not inside.

The completely healed eyes saw the darkness leave, the King entrust His spirit unto His Father, bow His head, and breathe His last (Luke 23:46; John 19:30). Bartimaeus would have seen that Someone opened the tombs immediately after the death of Jesus (Matt. 27:52). But with any true disciple of Jesus who was present that day, the story did not end there—for Jesus or for the redeemed. Because Bartimaeus was one of only two people specifically mentioned by name in Mark's Gospel, and because the home of Mark was a gathering place for Christians in Jerusalem and was the home to which Peter went when an angel released him from prison (Acts

12:12), that Mark specifically called him by name meant that the companion of Jesus who had received his sight must have been familiar to the home church in Jerusalem. Bartimaeus may very well have been among the more than 500 brethren to whom Jesus appeared at one time shortly after His resurrection (1 Cor. 15:6).

While not recorded in Scripture, we know that Bartimaeus would go the way of all fallen humanity (other than a few exceptions) and would eventually die. We will have to wait until we get to heaven to hear him and countless others tell the full story of their eternity-altering encounter with Jesus. Bartimaeus would encounter the temporary shroud of darkness at his death to be immediately followed by the opening of new eyes—again—in the presence of His friend, His Savior, and his eternal Companion, whose way led ultimately into the joyous eternal Glory of the Godhead face-to-face.

CHAPTER SEVEN

THE HIDING

We have seen in previous chapters, in what is incorrectly called "Aaron's Blessing," or "the Aaronic Blessing," that it is really God's blessing by means of Aaron. These were *God's words* communicated to the people by the high priest. As we also saw, when God gave the means and the terms of His blessing in Numbers 6:22–27, two of the six items, or one-third, were directly related to His face, initially to "shine on you" (Num. 6:25), followed by to "lift up His face/countenance on you." Both times action verbs are related to His face: "shine on" and "lift up." The obvious inference to make is that although God desires to bless, this blessing never merely happens by itself; God always requires specific actions in order to receive His blessing, even if it is simply receiving a grace gift from Him. And while there are other verses throughout the rest of Scripture that teach virtually the same thing, one crucial component of this doctrine cannot be stressed enough: *the original blessing given in Numbers 6:22–27 was to the nation of Israel, not to the Gentiles, or even to individual Jews*. This, of course, does not mean that God will not bless the Gentiles or that individual Jews could not receive aspects of this blessing. But it does mean that these collective six promises were at this point uniquely given to the Jewish people—nationally.

The context of Numbers 6 makes this abundantly clear. As we have already seen in our studies, and briefly by way of reminder, God had brought the newly redeemed Jewish people to Mount

Sinai (Ex. 19), where they remained until Numbers 10:11 (see also Lev. 27:34 and Num. 1:1). So from Exodus 19 until Numbers 10:11 the nation had not moved geographically. It was during this section that God and the people ratified what would come to be known as the Mosaic Covenant or "The Law of Moses," or just simply "the Law" (Ex. 24:1–8). "All the words which the LORD has spoken we will do!" (Ex. 24:3), and "All that the LORD has spoken we will do, and we will be obedient!" (Ex. 24:7) was a well-intended but utterly short-lived national promise before Yahweh concerning the nation's obedience to Him. They themselves had entered into a binding covenant relationship with the God who had brought them out of Egypt and who was in the process of bringing them back to the land He had previously promised them in the Abrahamic Covenant (Gen. 15:12–21). So when Moses was on Mount Sinai with God, and the foolishly wicked nation assembled around Aaron in Exodus 32:1, saying, "Come, make us gods who will go before us; as for this Moses, the man who brought us up from here, we do not know what has happened to him," this is not "a momentary lapse in judgment," or "they were just having a bad day." This was sheer brazen covenant violations before Yahweh in having other gods (Ex. 20:1–3) and in having idols (Ex. 24:4). If Aaron or one of the leaders had quoted what God had promised in the following verses in this second of the Ten Commandments, perhaps this high-handed sin of rebellion would not have occurred: "You shall not worship them or serve them; for I, the LORD your God, am a jealous God, visiting the iniquity of the fathers on the children, on the third and the fourth generations of those who hate Me, but showing lovingkindness to thousands, to those who love Me and keep My commandments" (Ex. 24:5–6). But Israel did not listen, and the immediate result was that approximately three thousand people were slain that day for their rebellion (Ex. 32:28). Even worse than that, the chapter tells of an undisclosed number of people who were ultimately affected by this sin, as the jealous God indeed did visit the iniquity on the people, as He had promised that he would. This chapter sadly concludes with, "Then the LORD smote the people, because of what they did with the calf that Aaron had made" (Ex. 32:35).

By the time God gave His blessing in Numbers 6, and again with the nation still encamped at the base of Mount Sinai, God had already established the Levitical priesthood through Aaron's lineage, with Aaron becoming the nation's first high priest (Ex. 28). Also, as we have seen, the LORD had given His two-options-only commands to the Jewish people of "Be obedient to Me, and I will bless you" (Lev. 26:1–13), or "Be disobedient to Me, and I will curse you" (Lev. 26:14–39). Obviously, everything in these chapters relates to the Jewish nation, and this would include the blessing that God offered in Numbers 6:22–27. This is important for the sheer fact that the blessing was *never* automatic for the Jewish people. Although it was the LORD's desire to bless, it was always contingent on the nation's obedient relationship to Him—or lack thereof—that would determine whether He would indeed "make His face shine on you" and "lift up His face/countenance on you, and give you peace" (Num. 6:25–26). As we have previously seen in our study, these wonderful blessings all result from living in a proper relationship with God, not in some good luck whim of fortune. And just by way of a quick reminder is God's requirement and promise that concludes this blessing, "So they shall invoke My name on the sons of Israel, and then I will bless them" (Num. 6:27).

Sadly, as the unfolding of God's progressive revelation repeatedly bore witness, the nation of Israel repeatedly sinned against their covenant-making and covenant-keeping God. So it should not be surprising that if the blessing of God required the presence of His face directly shining on the people and His face lifted up on them, the curse from God would have His face doing exactly the opposite, namely hiding from the people, which is precisely what Scripture teaches.

And so foundational is this doctrinal truth that we must emphasize this again and again: *there is no true, long-term blessing from God without the proper covenant relationship with and total obedience to Him.* If the nation of Israel—and later the Gentiles—had any desire for true blessing, it always flowed from their relationship to God. Attempting to gain His blessings without seeking His face was and is ultimately a futile endeavor, although it is by far the most common response around the much of what is called "the Christian world."

The opposite of God's desirous blessing for the Jewish people in Numbers 6:22–27 can readily be seen in other passages in the Pentateuch. After another brazen rebellion in Numbers 13–14, when the spies returned with an evil report and God sentenced that generation to die in the wilderness because of their sin, and after giving "the blessing and the curse" in Deuteronomy 28 to their children poised to go into the land that God had given them, God warned what would happen to this generation and future generations who rebelled against Him: "Then My anger will be kindled against them in that day, and I will forsake them *and hide My face from them*, and they shall be consumed, and many evils and troubles shall come upon them; so that they will say in that day, 'Is it not because our God is not among us that these evils have come upon us?' *But I will surely hide My face in that day* because of all the evil which they will do, for they will turn to other gods" (Deut. 31:17–18). Twice in this section God promised to hide His face in judgment if the people provoked Him because of their sin. Further, in the next chapter of Deuteronomy 32, God promised this for the Jewish nation who would "neglect the Rock of their salvation" in what is called the Song of Moses. God wanted the people to learn this divinely inspired song as a witness against them, and as would be expected, it would involve again His face:

> And the LORD saw this, and spurned them because of the provocation of His sons and daughters. Then He said, "*I*

will hide My face from them, I will see what their end shall be; for they are a perverse generation, sons in whom is no faithfulness. They have made Me jealous with what is not God; they have provoked Me to anger with their idols. So I will make them jealous with those who are not a people; I will provoke them to anger with a foolish nation, for a fire is kindled in My anger, and burns to the lowest part of Sheol, and consumes the earth with its yield, and sets on fire the foundations of the mountains. I will heap misfortunes on them; I will use My arrows on them" (Deut. 32:19–23).

An example of God's turning His face away in judgment due to the sins of the people as He promised He would do in Deuteronomy, especially in this context of the sinful rulers of the people, occurred centuries later in Micah 3:1–4:

And I said, "Hear now, heads of Jacob and rulers of the house of Israel. Is it not for you to know justice? You who hate good and love evil, who tear off their skin from them and their flesh from their bones, and who eat the flesh of my people, strip off their skin from them, break their bones, and chop them up as for the pot and as meat in a kettle." Then they will cry out to the LORD, but He will not answer them. Instead, *He will hide His face from them at that time*, because they have practiced evil deeds.

This should not have been surprising to the people, but usually those so ensnared in their rebellion do not truly believe that God will keep His word—that He will indeed severely judge—but indeed He will, precisely as He has repeatedly promised. The ones to whom Micah wrote were just as much under the Mosaic Covenant obligations as their forefathers had been in Exodus 24. Many other Bible examples exist that show God being gracious even after such sins, when the leaders and the people genuinely did repent before Him and amend their ways. However, if they did not turn from their sin, the Jewish people could expect God's hiding His face from them in judgment against their multiple and wicked covenant violations before Him.

Obviously, the blessings of Numbers 6 involving His face and the curses of Deuteronomy regarding hiding His face cannot occur at the same time, and as before, it is an "either-or" proposition. So for the nation of Israel, only two true options existed for the people, and both ultimately and directly related to the face of God: either He would shine His face upon them and lift up His face on them, or else He would turn His face away in judgment. Or stated differently, from Deuteronomy onward in every incident in Joshua, Judges, Samuel, Kings, or Chronicles, *every* event for the nation of Israel was directly due to either God's turning His face toward or away from His people. Most people would only observe the physical aspects of either blessing (such as during the early part of King David's reign) or severe judgment (such as the Exile in 586 B.C. during Zedekiah's reign). Yet the spiritual reality that God repeatedly presented in His Word is this: nothing happened by chance or fortune; He alone made—and makes—it happen. Whether this was or is acknowledged by people is irrelevant to the fact that God is the ultimate source, and God knows this. One day at the final judgment by God, everyone will know in full that God alone has done exactly has He has promised.

For individuals who love God, however, and often for those going through intense times of stress or affliction, the Bible contains the term "hide Your face" ten times used in reference to God. Unlike the judgment passages in Deuteronomy or Micah, these plaintive, beleaguered souls implored the God they love and trust on a personal basis, but from their perspective and due to their heavy burdens, considered that His face was hidden from them. A sampling of these verses shows this. We first see this in Job 13:24 where Job petitions God in his utter misery, "Why do you hide Your face and consider me Your enemy?" David prayed in Psalm 27:9, "Do not hide Your face from me, do not turn Your Servant away in anger; You have been my help; do not abandon me nor forsake me, O God of my salvation!" In a sad, poignant reversal, David actually prayed the opposite in Psalm 51:9: that God would "hide Your face from my sins," and the subscription of Psalm 51 shows that this was in response to Nathan the prophet rebuking David for his sins related to Bathsheba and Uriah the Hittite. Implied or directly stated in these intense prayers for the God they love to intervene and rescue is the since-the-Fall, perpetually nagging question of "why?" Psalm 88:14 states," O LORD, why do you reject my soul? Why do you hide Your face from me?" And finally, in Psalm 143:7, David pleaded, "Answer me quickly, O LORD, my spirit fails; do not hide Your face from me, lest I become like those who go down to the pit" [i.e. death]. God's interventions in these requests are evident in some of the pages in Scripture; how He has intervened in the past and will intervene in the future will be revealed at the future judgments of the LORD: "Therefore do not go on passing judgment before the time, but wait until the Lord comes who will both bring to light the things hidden in the darkness and disclose the motives of men's hearts; and then each man's praise will come to him from God" (1 Cor. 4:5).

The redeemed of Israel who walked in obedience, often in the midst of a majority of Jewish people who were living as a blatantly disobedient people, cried out not for the favor of God on them personally, but rather on the nation. Psalm 80 is such a psalm with three times the phrase "O God" [once] or "O God of hosts [twice], restore us [national Israel], and cause Your face to shine upon us, and we will be saved" (Ps. 80:3, 7, and 19). Obviously, this petition is based on the stated blessing of Numbers 6. However, as we have seen, such blessing from God is contingent on the entire nation turning away from their sin and turning to Him in obedience.

Many Bible readers have concluded that this blessing is a biblical impossibility because the Jewish people as a nation will *never* repent and obey. By these Bible readers' way of thinking, God is completely finished with national Israel due to their covenant violations culminating with the death of her rejected Messiah Jesus. However, God has already repeatedly stated what He would do in the future specifically in reference to His face and His Messiah—and to His Glory.

◆ ◆ ◆ ◆ ◆ ◆ ◆

One of my favorite classes that I teach at The Master's Seminary is Samuel/Kings/Chronicles. Each is one book in the Hebrew Bible; for instance, there is no First and Second Samuel in the Jewish Bible, only Samuel. Very broad indeed is the timeframe of these books as it transitions from the last judge, the prophet Samuel, to the first king Saul, to Saul's rejection by God and replacement with David, to the Davidic Covenant, to the separation of the ten northern tribes Israel and the two southern tribes Judah, to the exile of Israel to Assyria (722 B.C.), and finally to the destruction of Jerusalem and God's Temple by Nebuchadnezzar, king of Babylon, and the prophesied exile during the reign of King Zedekiah, the last man to sit on David's throne (586 B.C.).

Among other items, we begin our class with two very important points. First, these books are usually listed under the category of "Historical Books" in most Bibles or theology books—and that is far from the best designation. These books contain God-given doctrine, as does ultimately all of Scripture, as 2 Timothy 3:16–17 reveals: "All Scripture [including Samuel, Kings, and Chronicles] is inspired by God and profitable for teaching, for reproof, for correction, for training in righteousness; that the man of God may be adequate, equipped for every good work." Although these books most certainly do contain accounts of historical people and events, to categorize them as "Historical" renders them to be primarily talking about relatively irrelevant history (for some) instead of books that repeatedly show God's covenant faithfulness and His sovereignty, including some very important Messianic prophecies. For instance, the Davidic Covenant is first described in 2 Samuel 7; to limit this eternally important covenant of God as "Historical" would greatly affect one's interpretation of the Bible. Likewise, Chronicles is not a merely a repeat of Kings, but repeatedly gives a theological assessment of what God did and why, especially as it related to the blessing and the curse of Mosaic Covenant and the eternal promises that God had made with the Abrahamic and Davidic Covenants—and with a pointing to the New Covenant that God would make at some undisclosed time in the future.

If time permits in these classes, first, we try to line up the prophets of the Bible with the kings in whose reigns they ministered, with the vast majority of the writing prophets having ministered during this extended period. So not only can we find prophecy within these books, we can also see how God raised up specific prophets during this period. But of equal importance, we can see what God has promised to do in the future and very often why He will do it. Second, and connected to the first, I inform the class that if we start with the Exile, most people will conclude as the prophet Habakkuk did in the first chapter of his book, "How could God allow such a devastating event?" But if we start with God and His Word, specifically the blessing and the curse section of Leviticus 26 and Deuteronomy 28 and read the repeated, on-going wickedness and multiple covenant violations by the people, we usually wonder what took God so long as king after king and generation after generation lived in brazen covenant disobedience before Yahweh. In the southern kingdom Judah, and under some of the sons of David, national repentance followed by the resulting blessing of God would occur (such as during Hezekiah's reign), with God once more being word-for-word true to what He had promised. Sadly, however, the revivals were short lived, and the nation would soon return to their downward spiritual spiral that ultimately led to the exiles that God had already promised He would bring about.

So if one designates these books as strictly the "Historical Books," one would look for only ancient history instead of the progressive revelation of God that not only recorded accurately the historical events, but also contained prophecies about both the near and future times, especially for the Jews. For instance, Chronicles ends with a reminder of the blessed prophecy of God by means of Isaiah with a Gentile King Cyrus who would allow a remnant to leave Persia [modern day Iran] and return to the land of Israel to rebuild the Temple of God (Isa. 44:24–45:7; 2 Chron. 36:22–23; Ezra 1:1–4). For those who read and love God's Word, this requires no special hermeneutic to understand this Scripture as the Author of History brought into reality a Gentile king who would accomplish His sovereign will regarding the rebuilding of Jerusalem and God's own Temple. If one had known God's Scripture—and believed them—as the Babylonian exile came to an end, one should have been expecting a Gentile ruler named Cyrus to appear, about whom Isaiah prophesied long before the man was born, who would decree that God's Temple be rebuilt. And reading and believing God's Word is exactly what the godly prophet and exiled Jew Daniel did as he lived long enough to see Cyrus appear— exactly as God had promised: "And Daniel continued until the first year of Cyrus the king" (Dan. 1:21; see also 6:28; 10:1).

How thrilling it must have been for the elderly-by-this-time Daniel to live at the end of the seventy years exile that God had promised and to see the work that God was about to perform:

> In the first year of Darius the son of Ahasuerus, of Median descent, who was made king over the kingdom

of the Chaldeans—in the first year of his reign I, Daniel, observed in the books the number of the years which was revealed as the word of the LORD to Jeremiah the prophet for the completion of the desolations of Jerusalem, namely, seventy years. So I gave my attention to the Lord God to seek Him by prayer and supplications, with fasting, sackcloth, and ashes (Dan. 9:1–3).

Daniel confessed that the nation had sinned against Yahweh (Dan. 9:5–10) resulting with God being true to His Word "so the curse [Lev. 26/Deut. 28] has been poured out on us" (Dan. 9:11). But the true burden of this godly, dear prophet specifically regarded God's city Jerusalem and God's Temple:

> "And now, O Lord our God, who have brought Your people out of the land of Egypt with a mighty hand and have made a name for Yourself, as it is this day—we have sinned, we have been wicked. O Lord, in accordance with all Your righteous acts, let now Your anger and Your wrath turn away from Your city Jerusalem, Your holy mountain; for because of our sins and the iniquities of our fathers, Jerusalem and Your people have become a reproach to all those around us.
>
> "So now, our God, listen to the prayer of Your servant and to his supplications, and for Your sake, O Lord, let Your face shine on Your desolate sanctuary.
>
> "O my God, incline Your ear and hear! Open Your eyes and see our desolations and the city which is called by Your name; for we are not presenting our supplications before You on account of any merits of our own, but on account of Your great compassion. O Lord, hear! O Lord, forgive! O Lord, listen and take action! For Your own sake,

O my God, do not delay, because Your city and Your people are called by Your name" (Dan. 9:15–19).

Daniel 9:17 contains the plea, "let Your face shine on Your desolate sanctuary," directly based on the promised blessing of Numbers 6. There is much, much more in this account, especially as we see how it relates to the future in Daniel 9:24–27, with the coming signing of a strong covenant between the Antichrist and Israel to start anew the Temple sacrifices during the Tribulation. But at the very least, it is essential to understand that Daniel based his prayer, and then God answered based on a literal understanding of the previous prophecies of God. Not a trace of some allegorical or mystical understanding of either what God had promised or what He was about to do is evident in the text.

So was Daniel's prayer answered? Or stated differently, does God offer any word specifically regarding His face in the future—especially as it relates to Jerusalem, the Jewish people, and God's Temple?

♦ ♦ ♦ ♦ ♦ ♦ ♦

The prophets Isaiah, Micah and Hosea all ministered at approximately the same time ranging from somewhere around 755 B.C. to around 710 B.C. We should note that the first exile, that of the ten northern tribes of Israel taken into exile by Assyria, occurred during this time in 722 B.C. As horrendous an event that this would have been to witness, each godly prophet knew that God had previously very specifically promised exile in "the Blessing and the Curse," and because of the nation's repeated covenant violations, they would be severely judged by God.

It is most likely that all three prophets knew one another and perhaps were friends. For one thing, the land of Israel is not very large, so they were within just a day or two of one another wherever they were. Also, in a nation that lived in rebellion before God, the righteous remnant that God always preserved (Isa. 6:13)—which included at the time these three prophets—would always have a base of fellowship that those who had spurned God and His Word could not have. Simply put, they were on the same team and of the same theological mind, which sadly was not and is not always common. How much contact they would have had, we do not know. We do know that Hosea ministered to the northern tribes of Israel before they fell, and Isaiah and Micah ministered to the southern Kingdom of Judah, which had the Davidic Covenant heirs reigning.

So what did these prophets prophesy concerning the future of the nation of Israel and its relationship to their God? The same God who had promised in Micah 3:4, "Then they [the wicked leaders of the rebellious nation] will cry out to the LORD, but He will not answer them. Instead, He will hide His face from them at that time, because they have practiced evil deeds," gives hope that this is not an eternal hiding of His face. Even more specific, note the future blessings eternally recorded at the end of Micah's prophecy based on God's covenant faithfulness:

> Who is a God like You, who pardons iniquity and passes over the rebellious act of the remnant of His possession? He does not retain His anger forever, because He delights in unchanging love. He will again have compassion on us; He will tread our iniquities under foot. Yes, You will cast all their sins into the depths of the sea. You will give truth to Jacob and unchanging love to Abraham, which You did swear to our forefathers from the days of old (Micah 7:18–20).

The prophet Hosea would wholeheartedly concur with this teaching by revealing the future of national Israel regarding a prolonged vacancy of David's throne, followed by the advent of the One who would eventually come: "For the sons of Israel will remain for many days without king or prince, without sacrifice or sacred pillar, and without ephod or household idols. Afterward the sons of Israel will return and seek the LORD their God and David their king; and they will come trembling to the LORD and to His goodness in the last days" (Hos. 3:4–5).

When Hosea prophesied this, both Israel and Judah had kings reigning in the two countries; they had not yet remained "many days without king or prince." Even though Hosea ministered to the ten northern tribes, he, too, was a Jew who looked for the fulfillment of the Davidic Covenant. The prophetic nature beyond the immediate events is clearly seen in the phrase that concludes this prophecy, noting that this will occur "in the last days" (Hos. 3:5). God explains both the reason for His absence as well as the future remedy, promising in Hosea 5:15: "I will go away and return to My place until they acknowledge their guilt *and seek My face*; in their affliction they will earnestly seek Me." The prophet Isaiah also presents God in a prophecy as looking back on what He did to Israel and why, and how in His utter covenant faithfulness He will restore fellowship with the same Jewish nation He had previously punished, stating in Isaiah 54:7–10: "In an outburst of anger *I hid My face from you for a moment*; but with everlasting lovingkindness I will have compassion on you," says the LORD your Redeemer. "For this is like the days of Noah to Me; when I swore that the waters of Noah should not flood the earth again, so I have sworn that I will not be angry with you, nor will I rebuke you. For the mountains may be removed and the hills may shake, but My lovingkindness will not be removed from you, and My covenant of peace will not be shaken," says the LORD who has compassion on you.

The two-part requirements for national covenant renewal for the Jewish people and God's blessing are just as valid today as when He first gave them: (1) "they acknowledge their guilt," nationally acknowledged, as Daniel had previously done on an individual basis in Daniel 9, and (2) equally important, the nation must "seek My face." For those who insist that this will never happen, God insists, "in their affliction they will seek Me." This prophecy remains currently unfulfilled, but that will not always be the case as the collective response of the people clearly shows in the immediate verses that follow, Hosea 6:1–3:

> "Come, let us return to the LORD. For He has torn us, but He will heal us; He has wounded us, but He will bandage us. He will revive us after two days; He will raise us up on the third day that we may live before Him. So let us know, let us press on to know the LORD. His going forth is as certain as the dawn; and He will come to us like the rain, like the spring rain watering the earth."

In the approximately one hundred and fifty years after the prophecies of Isaiah, Micah and Hosea, God raised up another prophet, Ezekiel, who was taken in the second deportation to Babylon in 597 B.C. and who ministered among a rebellious people even in exile. After denunciation of Israel's sins by verbal messages and by object lessons that the prophet did at God's command, warning the people that Jerusalem was indeed going to fall to the Babylonians due to the nation's horrible multiple covenant violations, a report eventually came to Ezekiel and the people that Jerusalem had indeed been destroyed (Ezek. 33:21). Amazingly, "the hand of the LORD had been upon me in the evening before the refugees came" (Ezek. 33:22), as God began an entirely new series of prophecies regarding the nation's future one day before news of Jerusalem's destruction would arrive. Gone were the denunciations and severe rebukes; now came promise after promise issued by God about the future of His Jewish people, His city, His Temple—and His Glory.

For time's sake we must skip over most of this prophetic section. However, the summary statement by God Himself in Ezekiel 39:25–29 points to what He has promised to do one day in the future:

> Therefore thus says the Lord God, "Now I shall restore the fortunes of Jacob, and have mercy on the whole house of Israel; and I shall be jealous for My holy name. And they shall forget their disgrace and all their treachery which they perpetrated against Me, when they live securely on their own land with no one to make them afraid. When I bring them back from the peoples and gather them from the lands of their enemies, then I shall be sanctified through them in the sight of the many nations. Then they will know that I am the Lord their God because I made them go into exile among the nations, and then gathered them again to their own land; and I will leave none of them there any longer.
>
> "And I will not hide My face from them any longer, for I shall have poured out My Spirit on the house of Israel," declares the Lord God.

Let us be sure that we mark the final statement of this prophecy: "'And I will not hide My face from them any longer, for I shall have poured out My Spirit on the house of Israel,' declares the Lord God" (Ezek. 39:29). To express this another way, God will again work to bring the nation of Israel into covenant obedience—but only after severe judgment by God in the Tribulation (Jer. 30:4–9; Zech. 13:8–9)—so that the blessings of Numbers 6:22–27 can come to the Jewish people with the Lord "making His face shine on them" and "lifting up His countenance on them," so that Numbers 6:27 can come about: "So they shall invoke My name on the sons of Israel, and I then will bless them."

But before these wonderful blessings would occur and God again would turn His face toward them, the Jewish people would once again tragically reject God and His Word as God would visit His people—resulting in His hiding of His face once more in judgment.

♦ ♦ ♦ ♦ ♦ ♦ ♦

The final public teaching by the One who had set His face resolutely like flint (Isa. 50:7; Luke 9:51) was to the Jewish nation who had, for the most part, rejected Him to be the Messiah. Some had indeed truly believed; most did not believe (John 1:11–13). His final public teaching came in two parts with each one giving specific details about how utterly tragic this rejection of the Messiah was for the nation.

The first part of the final public teaching came in John 12:27–36:

> "Now My soul has become troubled; and what shall I say, Father, save Me from this hour? But for this purpose I came to this hour. Father, glorify Thy name." There came therefore a voice out of heaven: "I have both glorified it, and will glorify it again."
>
> The multitude therefore, who stood by and heard it, were saying that it had thundered; others were saying, "An angel has spoken to Him."
>
> Jesus answered and said, "This voice has not come for My sake, but for your sakes. Now judgment is upon this world; now the ruler of this world shall be cast out. And I, if I be lifted up from the earth, will draw all men to Myself." But He was saying this to indicate the kind of death by which He was to die.
>
> The multitude therefore answered Him, "We have heard out of the Law that the Christ [Messiah] is to remain

forever; and how can You say, the Son of Man must be lifted up? Who is this Son of Man?"

Jesus therefore said to them, "For a little while longer the light is among you. Walk while you have the light, that darkness may not overtake you; he who walks in the darkness does not know where he goes. While you have the light, believe in the light, in order that you may become sons of light." These things Jesus spoke, and He departed and hid Himself from them.

As with many other such examples in the Old Testament, as this actually still was under Old Testament times (Gal. 4:4), the hiding of God is not good news (John 12:36). Jesus hid Himself because of the sin of the people, sin that was worse than the sin of the wilderness generation because God had given so much more Light by this time. John 12:37–40 explains:

> But though He had performed so many signs before them, yet they were not believing in Him; that the word of Isaiah the prophet might be fulfilled, which he spoke, "Lord, who has believed our report? And to whom has the arm of the Lord been revealed?" For this cause they could not believe, for Isaiah said again, "He has blinded their eyes, and He hardened their heart; lest they see with their eyes, and perceive with their heart, and be converted, and I heal them."

This last quote John used was from Isaiah 6, the chapter that began with Isaiah saying "I saw the Lord sitting on a throne, lofty and exalted (Isa. 6:1). The following verse of John 12:41 explains without any question whom God's prophet saw: "These things Isaiah said, because he saw His [the Messiah's] glory, and he spoke of Him." Isaiah did indeed see God: the pre-incarnate second member of the

Godhead and a visible aspect of His glory—and this is true for every Old Testament viewing of God, such as the fellowship meal with God in Exodus 24:9–11.

The second part of the final public teaching of Jesus came in Matthew 23:27–36, as He excoriated the scribes and Pharisees for their sinfulness:

> "Woe to you, scribes and Pharisees, hypocrites! For you are like whitewashed tombs which on the outside appear beautiful, but inside they are full of dead men's bones and all uncleanness. Even so you too outwardly appear righteous to men, but inwardly you are full of hypocrisy and lawlessness.
>
> "Woe to you, scribes and Pharisees, hypocrites! For you build the tombs of the prophets and adorn the monuments of the righteous, and say, 'If we had been living in the days of our fathers, we would not have been partners with them in shedding the blood of the prophets.' Consequently you bear witness against yourselves, that you are sons of those who murdered the prophets. Fill up then the measure of the guilt of your fathers. You serpents, you brood of vipers, how shall you escape the sentence of hell?
>
> "Therefore, behold, I am sending you prophets and wise men and scribes; some of them you will kill and crucify, and some of them you will scourge in your synagogues, and persecute from city to city, that upon you may fall the guilt of all the righteous blood shed on earth, from the blood of righteous Abel to the blood of Zechariah, the son of Berechiah, whom you murdered between the temple and the altar. Truly I say to you, all these things shall come upon this generation."

Then before His crucifixion, Jesus had given His final public words as the love-sick Messiah had shown His kind intention that He had desired for the Jewish nation—as well as His grief for the ongoing rejection of Him—plus what would happen in the future:

> "O Jerusalem, Jerusalem, who kills the prophets and stones those who are sent to her! How often I wanted to gather your children together, the way a hen gathers her chicks under her wings, and you were unwilling. Behold, your house is being left to you desolate! For I say to you, from now on you shall not see Me until you say, 'Blessed is He who comes in the name of the Lord!'" (Matt. 23:37–39)

For those who want more detail, you can go again to *The Stone and the Glory* to the chapters entitled "The Lesson"—Parts 1 and 2 to read about this tremendously significant quoting from Psalm 118 by Jesus.

Actually, the concluding words of Jesus harmonize perfectly with those of His prophets whom He had sent before Him. The composite of some of the previous Scripture clearly showed what was taking place—and why—and for how long. Both Hosea 5:15 and Matthew 23:39 and related prophecies contain a monumental word that should not be overlooked and certainly not omitted: "until." The nation would indeed be many days without prince or king *until* God responded in the latter days (Hos. 3:3–4). This One was getting ready to "go away and return to My place" (Hos. 5:15)—which happened to be at the right hand of the Father *until* His enemies be made a footstool for His feet (Ps. 110:1; Matt. 22:44; Heb. 1:13–14). The hiding by God, repeatedly prophesied in Scripture, would be "*until* they [the Jewish people] acknowledge their guilt and seek My face" (Hos. 5:15), and "*until* you [the Jewish people] say, 'Blessed is He who comes in the name of the Lord'" (Ps. 118:26; Matt. 23:39).

Jesus simply told what had already been divinely revealed centuries earlier in the Holy Word of God. For instance, David penned Psalm 24 that shows who can approach God, and proves the true identity of the Messiah:

> The earth is the LORD's, and all it contains, the world, and those who dwell in it, for He has founded it upon the seas and established it upon the rivers. Who may ascend into the hill of the LORD and who may stand in His holy place? He who has clean hands and a pure heart, who has not lifted up his soul to falsehood and has not sworn deceitfully, he shall receive a blessing from the LORD and righteousness from the God of his salvation. This is the generation of those who seek Him, who seek Your face—even Jacob. Selah.
>
> Lift up your heads, O gates, and be lifted up, O ancient doors, that the King of glory may come in! Who is the King of glory? The LORD strong and mighty, the LORD mighty in battle. Lift up your heads, O gates, and lift them up, O ancient doors, that the King of glory may come in!
>
> Who is this King of glory?
>
> The LORD of hosts, He is the King of glory. Selah.

This eschatological psalm has "The LORD of Hosts"—the same King, the LORD of Hosts whom Isaiah saw in Isaiah 6:5 (as we also saw in John 12:41) as the King of Glory will return to His own Temple. Psalm 24:6 also speaks of the Jewish "generation of those who seek Him, who seek Your face [*paneh*]—even Jacob." Obviously, neither of these events occurred during the First Advent of Jesus, as we have seen in multiple passages: He did not enter His Temple as the King of Glory, and the nation as a whole would not receive Him as King Messiah.

However, one future generation awaits this blessed promise from Yahweh. But before that transpires, God must deal with them in a way fit for their disobedience and to bring them back into proper covenant relationship with Him and the promised blessings He desires to give. Ezekiel 20:33 begins with this divine declaration concerning God and His relationship with Israel: "As I live," declares the Lord God, "surely with a mighty hand and with an outstretched arm and with wrath poured out, *I shall be king over you*"—which clearly affirms that the next one to sit on David's throne must also be a Godhead member, namely, Jesus the Messiah, son of David (the human part) and Son of God (the Godhead part).

Yet in order for the Lord of Hosts, the King of Glory to reign over them, Israel must encounter Him in the way He sees fit and deems necessary:

> "And I shall bring you out from the peoples and gather you from the lands where you are scattered, with a mighty hand and with an outstretched arm and with wrath poured out; and I shall bring you into the wilderness of the peoples, *and there I shall enter into judgment with you face to face [paneh to paneh]*. As I entered into judgment with your fathers in the wilderness of the land of Egypt, so I will enter into judgment with you," declares the Lord God. And I shall make you pass under the rod, and I shall bring you into the bond of the covenant; and I shall purge from you the rebels and those who transgress against Me; I shall bring them out of the land where they sojourn, but they will not enter the land of Israel. Thus you will know that I am the Lord.
>
> "As for you, O house of Israel," thus says the Lord God, "Go, serve everyone his idols; but later, you will surely listen to Me, and My holy name you will profane no longer with your gifts and with your idols. For on My holy mountain,

on the high mountain of Israel," declares the Lord GOD, "there the whole house of Israel, all of them, will serve Me in the land; there I shall accept them, and there I shall seek your contributions and the choicest of your gifts, with all your holy things" (Ezek. 20:34–40).

And then—and there—the survivors of the collective nation of Israel, then in New Covenant obedient relation with Him, will say in the truest sense, "Blessed is He who comes in the name of the LORD" as the divine hiding will be over forever.

CHAPTER EIGHT

THE CONSIDERATION

As we saw in previous chapters, God had presented His Son Jesus to Israel as her only prophesied and God-ordained King Messiah (e.g., Ps. 2; Ps. 110), but the Jewish people did not receive Him as such at His First Advent, just as is prophesied in God's Word, and this is supported many times by Scriptures including, among other places, Isaiah 49:7; Matthew 21:33–46. Consequently, He would indeed hide Himself and return to His own place until the Jewish people repented and sought His face (Hos. 5:15), leaving the Jewish people many days without king or prince (Hos. 3:5) until—and this is important—they first enter into a covenant relationship with the Antichrist during the Tribulation (Dan. 9:27; Matt. 24:15). However, Israel cannot be in covenant obedience with the Antichrist and Jesus Christ at the same time. Afterward, "in the last days," Israel will "seek the LORD their God and [the true Son of] David [Jesus] their king" (Hos. 3:5). Fortunately and graciously, God will eventually pour out His Holy Spirit on the previously disobedient Jewish remnant, probably during the midpoint of the Tribulation, when their sins will be forgiven and they will be restored again to covenant obedience to Yahweh.

In Zechariah 12:10, God promises, "And I will pour out on the house of David and on the inhabitants of Jerusalem, the Spirit of grace and of supplication, so that they will look on Me whom they have pierced; and they will mourn for Him, as one mourns for an only son, and they will weep bitterly over Him, like the bitter weeping over a first-born." Zechariah 13:1 adds, "In that day a fountain will be opened for the house of David and for the inhabitants of Jerusalem, for sin and for impurity," namely the blood of the New Covenant already shed by Jesus the Messiah. Zechariah 13:8–9 reveals the breadth—and limitations—of this initial God-ordained saving of a remnant of Jewish people during the Tribulation:

> "And it will come about in all the land," declares the LORD,
> "That two parts in it will be cut off and perish; but the third will be left in it.
> And I will bring the third part through the fire,
> Refine them as silver is refined,
> And test them as gold is tested.
> They will call on My name,
> And I will answer them;
> I will say, 'They are My people,'
> And they will say, 'The LORD is my God.'"

Remember the utter importance of the promised blessing that the Jewish remnant whom God will redeem will receive when "they will call on My name," becoming one of the base contingencies—and benefits—for God to begin fulfilling all the promises He has given in the "The LORD bless you and keep you" blessings. We saw in a previous chapter that the six items in what is wrongly called "Aaron's Blessing" (Num. 6:22–26) will occur only when, as Numbers 6:27 states, "So they [the redeemed of national Israel] shall invoke My name on the sons of Israel, and I then will bless them."

Finally, the Bible ties these events directly to Armageddon and the Second Coming of Jesus Christ to earth, as Zechariah 14:1–4 discloses:

> Behold, a day is coming for the LORD when the spoil taken from you will be divided among you. For I will gather all the nations against Jerusalem to battle, and the city will be captured, the houses plundered, the women ravished, and half of the city exiled, but the rest of the people will not be cut off from the city.
>
> Then the LORD will go forth and fight against those nations, as when He fights on a day of battle. And in that day His feet will stand on the Mount of Olives, which is in front of Jerusalem on the east; and the Mount of Olives will be split in its middle from east to west by a very large valley, so that half of the mountain will move toward the north and the other half toward the south.

At some time after God pours out the Spirit on the Jewish remnant, He Himself "will gather *all* the nations against Jerusalem to battle" (Zech. 14:2). Then the newly cleansed Jewish remnant will say from a singular heart of adoration, "Blessed is He who comes in the name of the LORD" (Matt. 23:39; Ps. 118:26). The fact that Jesus said that the nation of Israel would not see Him again "until you say..." relates only to the public ministry of Jesus and not to His eventual reign as Messiah on David's throne. All of these prophesies will eventually come true—plus many promises that are not listed here. Here are some important prophecies from God's Word that He must fulfill. Not only will God gather all the nations, He also promises in Zechariah 14:3, "Then the LORD will go forth and fight against those nations, as when He fights on a day of battle," with the initial place of His return not left to futile speculation: "And in that day His feet will stand on the Mount of Olives, which is in front of Jerusalem on the east" (Zech. 14:4).

When Jesus hid Himself (John 12:36) and went into seclusion for a brief time, that time did not preclude all that He would have to do in the future. Before He reigns, He must first redeem, as He previously said in Mark 10:45, "For even the Son of Man did not come to be served, but to serve, and to give His life a ransom for many." But He would accomplish redemption only at the extreme cost of drinking the Cup that the Father had given Him (John 18:11), which means *everything* required by God for the salvation of others. Many would see Him crucified, but only select ones were to see Him resurrected, as Peter told Cornelius and his household, when the Gentiles were first receiving the Gospel offered to them on a broad basis, as Acts 10:39–41 states:

> "And we are witnesses of all the things He did both in the land of the Jews and in Jerusalem. And they also put Him to death by hanging Him on a cross. God raised Him up on the third day, and granted that He should become visible, not to all the people, but to witnesses who were chosen beforehand by God, that is, to us, [and similarly to the communal meal God served and partook of in Exodus 24:8–11] who ate and drank with Him after He arose from the dead."

God's Messiah had—and still has—many promises to keep and fully accomplish, as Jesus Himself promised in Matthew 5:18, "For truly I say to you, until heaven and earth pass away, not the smallest letter or stroke shall pass away from the Law, until all is accomplished."

The Gospel of Matthew that presents Jesus as the promised Christ/Messiah (identical meaning, John 1:41) was initially written primarily to a Jewish audience and was laced with Scripture from what we generally call the Old Testament (a name not used by Jews as a whole) to accurately substantiate Him that He alone was uniquely qualified—and remains uniquely qualified—as God's only Messiah. Scripture proves His unique qualifications with multiple verses predicting both the First Advent of the Messiah, His initial rejection—which God also prophesied with verses such as Psalm 118:22 ff. "the Stone that the builders have rejected has become the chief cornerstone" (Matt. 21:33–46)—and a larger number of verses that predict His Second Advent. Also, the Scriptural substantiation of Jesus as the Messiah, while prevalent in the Gospel of Matthew, is not exclusive to this book. The Godhead had already placed hundreds of verses throughout His Word about the Messiah's work and His Kingdom reign. It is still true today; nothing has changed about Jesus being God's anointed (Ps. 2:2) who currently sits at the right hand of the Father waiting for His enemies to be made a footstool for His feet at His Second Coming into His world to claim everything that is rightfully His—including His total vanquishing of His enemies (Ps. 110:1; Matt. 22:41–46; Heb. 1:13–14)—both human and demonic.

✦ ✦ ✦ ✦ ✦ ✦ ✦

John 5 presents an example of how Jesus viewed the Bible, with the context of this chapter showing the core problem of utter disbelief by most of the religious leaders. Jesus had healed on the Sabbath with the result: "And for this reason the Jews were persecuting Him [an imperfect tense in the Greek denoting repeated action; "they were repeatedly persecuting Him"] because He was doing these things on the Sabbath" (John 5:16), which was contrary only to their man-made tradition—but not to the requirements of God's Holy Word. To an already infuriated hostile assemblage of religious leaders, Jesus answered them in a way that would enrage them further by declaring, "My Father is working until now [a present tense denoting a continuous, on-going work that both the Father], and I Myself am working [likewise a present tense]" (John 5:17), even on the Sabbath that the Godhead had decreed and sanctified (Ex. 20:11). Obviously, the Father had no hostility toward Jesus about His actions on the

Sabbath. Even Nicodemus who was a Pharisee, a ruler of the Jews, had earlier deduced "Rabbi, we know You have come from God as a teacher; for no one could do these signs that you do unless God is with him" (John 3:1–2).

Notice that Jesus specifically qualified and restricted what He said in using the name "My Father." Shortly thereafter, He would tell His disciples to pray using the designation "Our Father who is in heaven," in the Disciples' Prayer (commonly referred to as the Lord's Prayer) during the Sermon on the Mount (Matt. 6:9). If the Jews who opposed Jesus needed anything else to enflame their hatred of Him even hotter than it already was, another encounter later in John 8:44–47 would more than suffice in Jesus' excoriating denunciation of those who were hostile to Him and in His accurate description of their true father:

> "You are of your father the devil, and you want to do the desires of your father. He was a murderer from the beginning, and does not stand in the truth, because there is no truth in him. Whenever he speaks a lie, he speaks from his own nature; for he is a liar, and the father of lies. But because I speak the truth, you do not believe Me. Which one of you convicts Me of sin? If I speak truth, why do you not believe Me? He who is of God hears the words of God; for this reason you do not hear them, because you are not of God."

Note again the hostile response to Jesus in John 8:48: "The Jews answered and said to Him, 'Do we not say rightly that you are a Samaritan and have a demon?'" By their way of reasoning, being a Samaritan would indicate His alleged illegitimate birth, making Him half-Jew and half-Gentile and thus permanently disqualifying Him from being "Son of David." Being a demoniac would show His origin from and influence by—if not full allegiance to—Satan, and obviously, these characteristics would designate someone who was unclean before them and God. Labeling Him a demoniac was a false accusation that Jesus Himself—or one of His parents—had committed some deeply sinful activity (or activities) in order for Him to have become such a demon possessed individual.

The hostility of the Jewish leaders to Jesus is shown further in the John 5 account. After Jesus identified the source of His work as being "My Father," these enemies of God responded accordingly: "For this cause therefore the Jews were seeking all the more to kill Him, because He not only was breaking the Sabbath, but also He was calling God His own Father, making Himself equal with God" (John 5:18). Jesus further stated in John 5:39, "You search the Scriptures because you think that in them you have eternal life; and it is these that bear witness of Me." As we saw, Jesus did not say, "You search the Old Testament," because at that time no one would have known what He meant, although He was certainly referring to what we now call the Old Testament; these inspired books were—and remain—part of "the Scriptures." The designation of Old Testament and New Testament would be a man-made division occurring centuries later, based on, among other things, chapters such as Hebrews 8. It is not incorrect to have man-made divisions, but it certainly is misleading, and often these divisions lead people to erroneously conclude that "Old" means ancient, out of date, and irrelevant to the New Testament church (and in certain cases this is true, especially as they relate to such practices as those in the Mosaic Covenant; see Acts 15 for two such dilemmas the Jerusalem Council faced), and "New" means important and relevant. Paul instructed Timothy and all others who read the Bible about the importance of these eternal words from the eternal God: "You, however, continue in the things you have learned and become convinced of, knowing from whom you have learned them; and that from childhood you have known the sacred writings which are able to give you the wisdom that leads to salvation through faith which is in Christ [Messiah] Jesus" (2 Tim. 3:14–15). "The sacred writings" would be what people now call the Old Testament. The eternal importance of these is clearly seen in the two verses that follow: "*All* Scripture is inspired by God and profitable for teaching, for reproof, for correction, for training in righteousness; that the man of God may be adequate, equipped for every good work" (2 Tim. 3:16–17)—even in the books contained in "the Old Testament."

Accordingly, many people begin their study of the Bible in Matthew 1 instead of Genesis 1. However, this leads to many problems in rightly dividing the Word of God. For example, one tremendously important time marker affects understanding the chronology of God's Word: Galatians 4:4–5: "But when the fulness of the time came, God sent forth His Son, born of a woman, born under the Law [the Mosaic Covenant], in order that He might redeem those who were under the Law [the Mosaic Covenant], that we might receive the adoption as sons." Among many others, three crucial deductions can be made from these verses. First, although "The New Testament" has Matthew 1:1 as its opening verse, technically speaking the New Testament/New Covenant would not be ratified until the death of Jesus (Luke 22:14–20)—not at His birth. The Temple veil that restricted access to the Holy of Holies, which came into being as part of God's original design under the Mosaic Covenant, was torn from top to bottom only after He cried out "It is finished!" (John 19:30). So actually, these and other parallel verses in the Gospels prove that the New Covenant begins at His death, not in Matthew 1/Mark 1/Luke 1 or John 1. Or stated differently, Matthew 1:1–27:51 is definitely included in "Old Testament times" under the Mosaic Covenant that was ratified in Exodus 24:1–8—including the life of Jesus—until the time when God Himself ratified the New Covenant with the blood of Jesus.

Second, we must emphasize how this understanding of when the New Covenant/New Testament (the words "covenant" and "testament" mean the same thing) gives us a more complete understanding of the Incarnation: Jesus lived *every* day of His life up to His death as a Jew under the strict requirements of the Mosaic Covenant—not the New Covenant—and He was held just as accountable to it as were Moses and the wilderness generation, Joshua, Saul, David, or any other Jew who was born from the time of Exodus 24 up to the inauguration of the New Covenant. Consequently, the relative of Jesus, John the Baptist, likewise was "born under the Law," and was, therefore, the last Old Testament prophet of God—not the first New Testament prophet.

Finally, when Satan tempted Jesus in the wilderness, he did so to One who "was born of a woman, born under the Law [the Mosaic Covenant]," and approached Him on that basis. Jesus did not answer as Incarnate God; every verse He quoted in response to the temptations was from the Torah in Deuteronomy, part of the Mosaic Covenant, as One "born under the Law." But there is much more to see in the life of Jesus, in the temptation under the law, and in what follows, all under the sovereign working of the Godhead.

♦ ♦ ♦ ♦ ♦ ♦

Satan's initial temptation of Jesus recorded in Matthew 4/Mark 1/Luke 4 occurred behind the scenes, totally away from public view, an event that was witnessed only by God and His angels, and most likely, also by Satan's angels of the demonic world (Matt. 25:41). If indeed the entire demonic world had watched this forty-day temptation, they would have been totally disheartened and devastated that not one of the temptations succeeded; Jesus refused every element of the enticements offered by Satan.

The composite accounts of Satan's initial temptation of Jesus give all the evidence that God wants us to know at the present time (Matt. 4:1–11; Mark 1:12–13; Luke 4:1–11). While many of us have read these accounts repeatedly, there are particulars that need to be considered in more detail, especially now that we know this temptation occurred "in Old Testament times." All three Gospels present different aspects of Jesus with each one based on the core theme that the author attempted to convey. Yet even while giving different details, a harmony remains among the three accounts. All three Gospels show Jesus' temptation by Satan taking place immediately following the baptism of Jesus—and this is important. Matthew 3:13–17 is such an account:

> Then Jesus arrived from Galilee at the Jordan coming to John, to be baptized by him. But John tried to prevent Him, saying, "I have need to be baptized by You, and do You come to me?" But Jesus answering said to him, "Permit it at this time; for in this way it is fitting for us to fulfill all righteousness." Then he permitted Him.
>
> And after being baptized, Jesus went up immediately from the water; and behold, the heavens were opened, and he saw the Spirit of God descending as a dove, and coming upon Him, and behold, a voice out of the heavens, saying, "This is My beloved Son, in whom I am well-pleased."

The baptism of Jesus was more than just a historical event; it identified Jesus with His Jewish people, namely the house of Israel. But beyond this, the baptism—and even more the response by the remaining members of the Godhead—specifically and officially designated Jesus as God's Messiah. After all, the word "Messiah" or "Christ" means "The Anointed One," and the baptism of Jesus was the time of His being anointed as Messiah. A specific anointing was fitting and required for every true King of Israel. For example, First Samuel 16:12–13 shows the prophet Samuel anointing David as Israel's new king:

> So he [Samuel] sent and brought him in. Now he [David] was ruddy, with beautiful eyes and a handsome appearance. And the LORD said, "Arise, anoint him; for this is he." Then Samuel took the horn of oil and anointed him in the midst of his brothers; and the Spirit of the LORD came mightily upon David from that day forward. And Samuel arose and went to Ramah.

Not only was David anointed, that is officially marked and designated as the new king of Israel, but he was also empowered by God to do all that was necessary as king as "the Spirit of God came mightily upon David from that day forward." Someone with the Spirit of God mightily upon him would do incredible works that only God's power alone could produce, and this is exactly what David did, especially in the early years of his actions as anointed king. But sadly, he did not rule perfectly, as was shown by his sins with Bathsheba and the horrible and on-going consequences of his divinely given punishment that would cause David crushing sorrow for the remainder of his life.

About one thousand years later, another Son of David (Matt. 1:1) was anointed—and it is fitting that the passive voice was always used. No true king would anoint himself; he had to be anointed by God's representative. But unlike the anointings of previous kings, eventually leading up to the last Son of David to sit on David's throne, King Zedekiah in 586 B.C., for the first time in about six hundred years, another Son of David was anointed, not only to become King, but also to become the Messiah, "the LORD's Anointed" (Ps. 2:2), and God's King, as seen in Psalm 2:6: "But as for Me, I have installed My King upon Zion, My holy mountain."

But everything about this One—and His anointing—differed from any other anointings that had ever occurred in the history of the world. To begin with, God Himself did the anointing, not the attending prophet of God who was at hand, namely John the Baptist. Also, God did not use oil to anoint Jesus; He used the third member of the Godhead, the Holy Spirit. So, all three members of the Godhead were present and active as God the Father anointed His beloved Son with the beloved Holy Spirit. Also, if previously the "Spirit came mightily on David from that day forward" from the anointing of this sinful, contaminated Son of Adam, how much more with this blessed and holy One who was—and ultimately always would be—sinlessly perfect. Furthermore, because Philippians 2:5–11 tells about Jesus completely "emptying Himself" of the free use of His attributes of God, He must be anointed with a capacity to do the mighty works of God that He would do. Jesus acknowledged this in Matthew 12:28 where Jesus countered His hostile foes with, "But if I cast out demons by the Spirit of God, then the kingdom of God has come upon you." Jesus was anointed at His baptism and empowered by the Spirit of God to do everything necessary to be the Messiah, as was seen as part of Peter's message to the Gentiles who were about to receive the same Gospel, in Acts 10:38, "You know of Jesus of Nazareth, how God anointed Him with the Holy Spirit and with power, and how He went about doing good, and healing all who were oppressed by the devil; for God was with Him." Logically, the Bible presents no miracles done by Jesus until after He was anointed—and empowered—by the Holy Spirit.

So a summarization of some points about Matthew's account of events leading to Jesus' temptation by Satan is important. First, "this is My beloved Son" marked Jesus uniquely as the Son of God—not only the Son of David, which we have already seen in Matthew 1 and Luke 1:30–33. Second, note the Spirit's regal leading of the newly anointed King Jesus, as the Spirit had just come upon Him at His Baptism as Matthew 4:1 states, "Then Jesus was led up by the Spirit into the wilderness to be tempted by the devil." Third—and this is important—God is the One who initiated this battle and this battlefield, not Satan. Satan did not have to search to find God's Son the King; God the Holy Spirit led the newly and permanently Anointed One/Messiah into the wilderness with the sole purpose that He would be tempted by Satan. One final thought: Matthew puts the emphasis on Jesus' fasting for forty days and nights and His becoming hungry, which was followed by the tempter coming to Him in this weakened-in-the-flesh condition.

After Jesus passed this particular trial, Matthew 4:11 reveals a truth we would not know from the other Gospel accounts: "Then the devil left Him, and behold angels came and began to minister to Him." As we have seen in other studies, the word "Behold!" translated as "Mark this!" "Pay attention!" should always be understood as having an exclamation point to show its importance. When Satan quoted Psalm 91:11–12 by noting "He will give His angels charge concerning You," God in fact did just that, but He waited until the end of this early temptation segment by Satan, not when Jesus was in the very midst of it.

The Gospel of Mark differs from Matthew in its presentation of Jesus as "the perfect Servant of Yahweh," and although He is seen in this way at various places throughout Scripture, this designation is especially detailed in the four "Servant Songs" of Isaiah (Isa. 42:1–9; 49:1–13; 50:4–11; 52:13–53:12). Mark's account of the temptation of Jesus is the briefest, but it includes unique material, all harmonizing with the composite picture that God intended:

> And it came about in those days that Jesus came from Nazareth in Galilee, and was baptized by John in the Jordan. And immediately coming up out of the water, He saw the heavens opening, and the Spirit like a dove

descending upon Him; and a voice came out of the heavens: "You [emphatic in the Greek] are My beloved Son, in You I am well-pleased." And immediately the Spirit impelled Him to go out into the wilderness. And He was in the wilderness forty days being tempted by Satan; and He was with the wild beasts, and the angels were ministering to Him (Mark 1:9–13).

Note the servant elements highlighted by Mark in contrast with the regal elements emphasized by Matthew. In Matthew 4:1 "the Spirit led Jesus into the wilderness;" in Mark's Gospel the Spirit "compelled Jesus," employing the same Greek word used throughout the Gospels for Jesus "casting out" demons. The King was led; the Servant was compelled, or even "thrown" into the wilderness. Mark adds the unique description that Jesus "was with the wild beasts." How many wild beasts were there and what they did, we are not told. The angels who ministered to Him in the midst of this anguishing time (Mark 1:13) may have been used by God to protect His Servant against such wild beasts that almost certainly were not the only ones who were hungry in the wilderness, but this One so well pleasing to the Father had no fear of death. To know whether or not the wild beasts caused Him any physical harm or disrupted any brief escape of sleep He may have enjoyed, we will have to wait for the Godhead's full disclosure in Heaven.

But Mark's Gospel adds another distinct description that is definitely worth noting. Both Matthew 3:16 and Luke 3:21 contain the normal Greek word for "open" in describing the heavens opening after Jesus' baptism. Mark did not. He used another word (*skidzo*) that is generally translated "to tear or to rip." This word occurs later in both Mark 15:38 and Matthew 27:51 to describe the Temple veil restricting the Holy of Holies as being torn open. But Mark first used this word of strong action at the baptism of Jesus. His account does not focus on the heavens opened—which they did—his emphasis was that they were torn open or even "ripped open." This violent ripping of heaven was God's opening challenge to Satan and to all who were hostile to God's Son, in total contrast to the gentleness of the Holy Spirit descending in the form of a dove, and was a mighty call to battle to the highly intensified spiritual warfare that was at hand.

Luke's Gospel presents Jesus as the perfect man, and accordingly, after the baptism, Luke 3:22 presents Jesus as "the son of God"—not Son of David—and the genealogy goes in descending order and directly connects Him with "Adam, the [first] son of God" (Luke 3:38), and to the defiling and disfiguring effects of the Fall on all humanity from Adam onward—except to Jesus. Thus the temptation account in Luke 4 begins the process of Jesus redeeming and reclaiming all that Adam had forfeited—and infinitely more.

Beyond this, Luke's Gospel reveals an essential truth that we would not know unless God had revealed it: "And when the devil had finished every temptation, he departed from Him until an opportune time" (Luke 4:13). Satan knew that he had utterly lost this initial battle, but also he considered that the ultimate war would be continuous; he would actively be seeking "an opportune time" to tempt Jesus or to make Him blunder in some way. Added to this, however, is an intriguing question that we need to ponder: did Satan employ *all* that was at his disposal in tempting Jesus in the Matthew 4/Mark 1/Luke 4 account, or did he reserve some demonic tactics to use later? From Luke's Gospel it was evident that the devil expected "a more opportune time" would be his, but it says nothing in regard to the resources available to Satan to use against Jesus. The account of the initial temptation gives no indication that Satan held back anything that was available to him at that time to employ in the first temptation. However, from nuggets contained within God's Word, we find that not only did an opportune time become available to Satan, but that also God granted Satan temporary access to

Jesus beyond his belief and in a most unexpected manner as it relates to the face of God.

♦ ♦ ♦ ♦ ♦ ♦ ♦

Luke 22 presents many behind-the-scenes truths that we otherwise would not know concerning the events related to the rapidly approaching crucifixion, with many of these truths in some way directly connected with Satan. For instance, Luke 22:1–4 reveals the following:

> Now the Feast of Unleavened Bread, which is called the Passover, was approaching. And the chief priests and the scribes were seeking how they might put Him to death; for they were afraid of the people.
>
> *And Satan entered into Judas* who was called Iscariot, belonging to the number of the twelve. And he went away and discussed with the chief priests and officers how he might betray Him to them.

We are not told exactly how many days it took for Satan residing inside Judas' body to make the necessary arrangements to betray Jesus, but at the very least it would have required a few days before the Feast of Unleavened Bread/Passover began.

All four Gospels contain a description of events related to Jesus and "the Last Supper," with the longest description given in John 13–17, often called "the Upper Room Discourse," which gives us additional biblical doctrine not found elsewhere in Scripture. When added with the other Gospel accounts, God has given us all that He wants us to know for the present time—but what biblical gold He left for us in His holy Word!

If one were reading the Bible for the first time, it should not be unexpected to see the love of Jesus in the pages of Scripture that describe so beautifully His wondrously sacrificial love, as John's account of the Last Supper begins with this beautiful description in John 13:1, "Now before the Feast of the Passover, Jesus knowing that His hour had come that He should depart out of this world to the Father, having loved His own who were in the world, He loved them to the end." Sadly, one should not be surprised to see Satan referred to again, especially with his earlier entrance into Judas, as we saw in Luke 22:1; John 13:2 follows with, "And during supper, the devil having already put into the heart of Judas Iscariot, the son of Simon, to betray Him." Then, the Holy Spirit by means of the human author John, pulls the focus away from Satan and back—properly—to Jesus, as seen in John 13:3-4: "Jesus, knowing that the Father had given all things into His hands, and that He had come forth from God, and was going back to God, rose from supper, and laid aside His garments; and taking a towel, He girded Himself about."

We must turn back and forth between two of the Gospels and among a few other passages as we follow God's biblical trail to achieve a greater understanding of the events—and prayerfully to increase more deeply our worship and adoration for Jesus. For instance, in Luke's account of the of the Last Supper, in the same context in which Jesus would first reveal what He would be accomplishing with the New Covenant that would be ratified in His blood the next day on the cross (Luke 22:14-20), Jesus took Peter aside to specifically warn him of what was about to happen—and to reveal the true source of this horrific, impending spiritual attack: "Simon, Simon, behold, Satan has demanded permission [received permission from God the Father] to sift you like wheat; but I have prayed for you, that your faith may not fail; and you, when once you have turned again, strengthen your brothers" (Luke 22:31-32). (Those who desire further details of this account can read the chapter entitled "The Surprise" in *The*

Cup and the Glory). While we cannot study every biblical truth here, we should note at least a few pertinent matters for our present study. Under a more leisurely setting over the previous years, Jesus might have added more about the coming occurrences—but the countdown to Calvary had officially begun, and the Divinely predetermined time of events left Jesus with only a limited time remaining.

When Peter heard Jesus' warning of what Satan was going to do to him, he should have been shaken to the uttermost core within him, because only two times in all of Scripture had God previously revealed anything similar to what Jesus warned Peter about, and the other times are found in Job 1–2. However, instead of heeding Jesus' words at that moment, Luke 22:33 uncovers Peter's pride during this part of his spiritual walk, and his false estimation of his own personal strength and resolve to resist evil, as well as his mammoth underestimating of the depth—and torture—of the satanic sifting that Jesus warned him of that would begin in only a few hours: "And he [Peter] said to Him, 'Lord, with You I am ready to go both to prison and to death!'"

Whether Peter's mind ever briefly flashed back to the contents of Job 1 and 2, we are not told, but we should return to these two chapters to gain some additional divine revelation that will factor into having a better understanding of the biblical account—and to develop a deeper love of God because of these truths. To begin with, the Book of Job is chronologically the first book written in the Bible, thus making the first two chapters of Job the first two chapters of the Bible (chronologically), and each of these chapters contains a different account of Satan appearing before God in heaven. Job 1:6 begins: "Now there was a day when the sons of God came to present themselves before the LORD, and Satan also came among them."

The term used here "the sons of God" can mean, depending on its context, the holy angels of God alone, and because this occurs in heaven and not on earth, this cannot be the sons of God with reference to anyone on earth that time, such as those earthly sons shown in the last verse of Jesus' genealogy in Luke 3:38: "the son of Enosh, the son of Seth, the son of Adam, the son of God." The sons of God who appear in heaven are not human beings, rather they are angelic beings. And beyond this, in the broader context of other Scripture—if God intends—the sons of God can widen in its description to include the unholy angels, who were at one time holy, but who followed Satan and permanently became his angels (Matt. 25:41; Rev. 12:3–4), who are more commonly referred to as demons. One reason we know that this can also refer to demons is that Satan came with the holy angels. Another reason we know is that when Satan and his angels are allowed—or even summoned—they have access to heaven, but they must stand below God's throne, obviously lower than the Godhead, and they must stay or come to heaven only to the degree that the holy Trinity sees fit. Revelation 12:7–9 reveals when and how during the Tribulation this present status will end:

> And there was war in heaven, Michael and his angels waging war with the dragon. And the dragon and his angels waged war, and they were not strong enough, and there was no longer a place found for them in heaven. And the great dragon was thrown down, the serpent of old who is called the devil and Satan, who deceives the whole world; he was thrown down to the earth, and his angels were thrown down with him.

These events await their God-ordained fulfillment in the future Tribulation. Until then, and only to the degree that God sees fit, Satan still has access to heaven; some of the other demons are already imprisoned by God in the abyss, and obviously, these demons would not be among the fallen "sons of God" who would have access to God in heaven (1 Pet. 3:17–19; 2 Pet. 2:4; Jude 6; and Rev. 9:1–12).

We must go back to the first two chapters of the Book of Job to see some biblical truths we will need to study later in this chapter. Just to be reminded of the context, we will start at the verse in Job that we have already studied and continue from there. Job 1:6–12 reveals:

> Now there was a day when the sons of God came to present themselves before the Lord, and Satan also came among them. And the Lord said to Satan, "From where do you come?" Then Satan answered the Lord and said, "From roaming about on the earth and walking around on it."
>
> And the Lord said to Satan, "Have you considered [literally "set your heart to"] My servant Job? For there is no one like him on the earth, a blameless and upright man, fearing God and turning away from evil."
>
> Then Satan answered the Lord, "Does Job fear God for nothing? Have you not made a hedge about him and his house and all that he has, on every side? You have blessed the work of his hands, and his possessions have increased in the land. But put forth Your hand now and touch all that he has; he will surely curse You to Your face [*paneh*]."
>
> Then the Lord said to Satan, "Behold, all that he has is in your power, only do not put forth your hand on him." So Satan departed from the presence [*paneh*] of the Lord.

Many who read this account fail to note one inarguable truth: Satan does not ask permission to attack Job; *God Himself* puts the challenge to Satan concerning His choice vessel Job, something which poor Job on earth would have completely been unaware of until the end of the book. That God would be the One who initiates these events that would so grievously decimate Job and his family biblically coincides later with Jesus being led by the Holy Spirit—not led by Satan—into the wilderness to be tested by the devil (e.g. Matt. 4:1). Also, the cursing of God to His face [*paneh*] is what Satan claims will assuredly be the outcome once the horrendous events have transpired and Job has had time for his consideration of the devastation that would come upon his family and his wealth. As seen earlier, but something still worth noting, is that Job 1:12 concludes with God establishing the parameters and degree that Satan may attack Job and his family, "Then the LORD said to Satan, 'Behold, all that he has is in your power, only do not put forth your hand on him.' So Satan departed from the presence [*paneh*] of the LORD."

Virtually all of the above elements occur also in the next episode between God and Satan, as seen in Job 2:1–7:

> Again there was a day when the sons of God came to present themselves before the LORD, and Satan also came among them to present himself before the LORD. And the LORD said to Satan, "Where have you come from?" Then Satan answered the LORD and said, "From roaming about on the earth, and walking around on it."
>
> And the LORD said to Satan, "Have you considered [the same verb used as before, literally "set your heart to"] My servant Job? For there is no one like him on the earth, a blameless and upright man fearing God and turning away from evil. And he still holds fast his integrity, although you incited Me against him, to ruin him without cause."
>
> And Satan answered the LORD and said, "Skin for skin! Yes, all that a man has he will give for his life. However, put forth Your hand, now, and touch his bone and his flesh; he will curse You to Your face [*paneh*]."
>
> So the LORD said to Satan, "Behold, he is in your power, only spare his life."

> Then Satan went out from the presence [*paneh*] of the LORD, and smote Job with sore boils from the sole of his foot to the crown of his head.

As with the first challenge, God is also the One Who initiates the second challenge for Satan to consider Job and for Satan to consider his utter failure in his first attack against Job. Again, Satan challenges God to remove His protective restriction from Job and to allow Satan to inflict such intensely severe physical pain that Job will then curse God to His face [*paneh*]. As God did before, He sets the limitations that Satan is not permitted to kill Job, only to severely torment him. Satan, in total failure, loses in his second bet with God in that even though Job is severely tormented, he does not curse God to His face.

Fast forward a few thousand years later to the accounts of that night of nights and the last Passover Jesus ever partook of until He returns to earth to reign:

> And when the hour had come He reclined at the table, and the apostles with Him. And He said to them, "I have earnestly desired to eat this Passover with you before I suffer; for I say to you, I shall never again eat it until it is fulfilled in the kingdom of God" (Luke 22:14–16).

However, the evening took an unexpected turn for all of them when Jesus unexpectedly dropped a prophetic doctrinal truth bombshell in their midst when He announced in John 13:21–25:

> When Jesus had said this, He became troubled in spirit, and testified, and said, "Truly, truly, I say to you, that one of you will betray Me." The disciples began looking at one another, at a loss to know of which one He was speaking.

> There was reclining on Jesus' breast one of His disciples, whom Jesus loved.
>
> Simon Peter therefore gestured to him, and said to him, "Tell us who it is of whom He is speaking." He, leaning back thus on Jesus' breast, said to Him, "Lord, who is it?"

In answering who among the disciples would betray Him, Jesus gives the answer that many of us are familiar with in John 13:26: "Jesus therefore answered, 'That is the one for whom I shall dip the morsel and give it to him.' So when He had dipped the morsel, He took and gave it to Judas, the son of Simon Iscariot." With everything we have seen from Luke 22 and the opening verses of John 13, we should not be a surprised by how Jesus answered. However, what transpires next reveals deep theological truths that we would not know existed unless God had revealed them, and even then, it is easy not to comprehend the magnitude of what the next verse reveals about Judas: "And after the morsel, *Satan then entered into him.* Jesus therefore said to him, 'What you do, do quickly" (John 13:27).

We have previously noted that Satan entered into Judas, but the Luke 22:1–4 passage occurred days before the Passover night and "the Last Supper:"

> Now the Feast of Unleavened Bread, which is called the Passover, was approaching. And the chief priests and the scribes were seeking how they might put Him to death; for they were afraid of the people.
>
> *And Satan entered into Judas* who was called Iscariot, belonging to the number of the twelve. And he went away and discussed with the chief priests and officers how he might betray Him to them.

Because Jesus' identification of the betrayer is so crucial to the overall crucifixion account, it is easy to miss the tremendously important part of John 13:27, namely that Satan entered into Judas a *second* time: "And after the morsel [that Jesus gave], *Satan then entered* [same word used days earlier in Luke 22:3] *into him* [Judas]." What many people who read the biblical account fail to note is that *there are actually two entrances of Satan into Judas—not one—and that they are days apart.*

Here stands before us the simple question that most people have not considered: *why did Satan enter into Judas twice in a matter of days, and is there anything we can learn from this that will add to our understanding of the events associated with the Last Supper?* Some argue to attempt to answer this question is only foolish speculation at best. God Himself does not view the account as an impossible endeavor to understand, but instead He gives us a better answer to these questions—plus why they are eternally important—in His holy Word that are definitely not speculations.

♦ ♦ ♦ ♦ ♦ ♦ ♦

Directly after Jesus had dismissed Judas from the last Supper, Jesus turned to Peter, as revealed in Luke 22:31–32: "Simon, Simon, behold, Satan has demanded permission to sift you like wheat; but I have prayed for you, that your faith may not fail; and you, when once you have turned again, strengthen your brothers."

We must pay careful attention to a few eternally important matters in additional divine revelation made by Jesus. First, Jesus used the important word "Behold!" (Mark this! Pay attention!) to open His remarks about Satan and what was about to happen. Second, Jesus used a second person plural "you" or "you all" in "Satan has demanded permission to sift you [plural] like wheat;" thus, all the Eleven would receive Satan's sifting to various degrees—not just Peter. However, Jesus switched to a second person singular "you" in

Luke 22:32 four times within this verse with each use directly related to Jesus' special prayer for Peter in spite of Peter's impending failure during his torturous spiritual sifting: "but I have prayed for *you*, that *your* faith may not fail; and *you*, when once you have turned again, strengthen *your* brothers"—all second person singular "you" or "yours." This distinction we would not see in our English Bible, but it clearly stands out in the Greek New Testament. Third, and very important for us to note in this account, is one simple fact: Jesus reported about what Satan had *already* received; no future tense verb is used to describe what will be granted to him. Satan had already received authority from God the Father that He alone could—and did—give to him, and Jesus knew full well that the enemy would soon violently attack these beloved sheep of the His own fold. We are not told exactly when Satan stood before God and received this required permission to do what he could never do by his own authority, but it reasons that it had to have been relatively recently, perhaps even earlier that very day or a few days earlier—as we will see in God's Word.

By knowing that Satan entered into Judas twice, one may ask the considerably simple but eternally profound question that can be biblically answered: *Why? Why did Satan enter into Judas twice?* Some people say that it would only be speculation if we tried to find the answer, but the Bible is clear about why Satan was forced to temporarily vacate Judas' body for a day or a few days, and then later reenter it: *Satan could not appear before the God the Father to make his request about the Eleven while he was still inside of Judas' body, and thus had to temporarily divest himself of it, so that Satan could make the appeal found Luke 22:31–32.* It is Jesus' knowledge of what Satan will do to the disciples that evokes such a such a strong warning from Jesus: "Simon, Simon, behold, Satan has demanded permission [already received permission from God the Father] to sift you like wheat; but I have prayed for you, that your faith may not fail; and you, when once you have turned again, strengthen your brothers" As was true for the account in Job

1–2, the appeal by Satan had to be made in heaven before God—not on earth—as clearly seen in Job 1:6, "Now there was a day when the sons of God came to present themselves before the LORD [in heaven], and Satan also came among them," and Job 2:1, "Again there was a day when the sons of God came to present themselves before the LORD [in heaven], and Satan also came among them to present himself before the LORD." In the Job 1–2 account, Satan appeared before the LORD in the spiritual body that God created for him. The same would be true of the Luke 22:31 appeal by Satan that Jesus revealed: "Simon, Simon, behold, Satan has demanded permission [received permission from God the Father] to sift you like wheat." Satan had to make this appeal in his same created spiritual form as he appeared before in Job 1–2, and certainly not while encased in Judas' body, but instead, in Satan's normative spiritual body created for him by God.

Everything about the appeal made by Satan in Luke 22:31 seems to have originated from him. Satan was the one who desired to sift the Eleven by extreme spiritual torment, and this verse clearly proves that if God the Father did not grant permission to Satan, then Satan would have no authority to spiritually sift them. This is one example of God's loving protection, but it also reveals that if God sees fit to grant Satan permission to inflict such carnage—physically or spiritually—Satan would most assuredly take advantage of what God permitted him to do.

We know from our earlier study that Satan asked—and received—permission to sift the Eleven (Luke 22:31). Later in Luke's account, at the arrest of Jesus, we are given vital information about another encounter in which Satan was granted a request that he made to God. We also know that in this same chapter, Jesus at His arrest revealed a startling truth not found elsewhere in Scripture, saying to Satan: "but this hour and the power of darkness are yours," or worded more literally, "but this is your hour, and the authority of the darkness is yours" (Luke 22:53). Satan had received an indescribable segment of time ("your hour") and "the authority of the darkness is yours" that went far beyond the initial request about the sifting of the Eleven. Never before had Satan received such power and authority. For instance, he did not have this authority given to him earlier in the 40-day temptation of Jesus in passages such as Luke 4:1–13. But, then again, how and when did Satan receive such authority? One of two things happened: either there was one meeting where Satan received the authority to spiritually sift Peter and the others, and then God gave Satan beyond what he had requested, namely "the hour of the authority of the darkness," or there were at least two meetings of Satan before God—such as occurs in Job 1–2—and the second meeting (if there were two meetings)—would be the time when Satan received the additional authority, previously not allowed for him about Jesus, "but this is your hour, and the authority of the darkness is yours." Whether one meeting or two meetings occurred where Satan appeared before God, Satan had to do this in his own demonic essence, and he did not do this from inhabiting the body of Judas. Shortly after Satan received his "authority of the darkness," at the proper and last time, Satan reentered the body of Judas during the Last Supper, as seen in John 13:27: "And after the morsel [that Jesus gave to Judas], Satan then entered into him [Judas]."

These are rare sobering thoughts to ponder as some of the cost of what Jesus would endure begins to become more evident, and yet there is still one more serious subject to consider: From the events disclosed in Luke 22, God Himself may have placed another consideration before Satan thousands of years after the ones He previously had given Satan in Job 1–2. We are not adding to scripture nor putting words into God's mouth, but if you were to change the name in Job 1:8 to "Jesus," everything would fit in infinite perfection, as Jesus' Incarnation was coming to an end: "And the LORD said to Satan, 'Have you considered [literally in the Hebrew, "set your heart to"] My servant Jesus? For there is no one like him on the earth, a blameless and upright man, fearing God and turning away from evil.'" God could further have added, "My Son, my only Son in whom I am well-pleased, perfectly abiding under the Mosaic Covenant under which He was born and living in perfect fellowship with Me." If just hours before Jesus would be crucified God did indeed become the initiator in this final meeting with Satan as He had initiated meetings twice before to Job in Job 1–2, then God offered Satan the most unexpected consideration that tremendously exceeded the initial 40-day temptation of Jesus or the pending sifting of the eleven: Satan's God-granted hour of the darkness given to him. Simply stated, Satan's "hour of authority the darkness" ultimately may have been God's idea—not even Satan's request.

If this is true, it would give understandable clarifications for many events. For instance, not that God is under obligation to justify Himself to anyone, it would answer the critics who question why God could have allowed such horrendous satanic attacks against Job and his family in Job 1–2 knowing that the attacks would be unspeakably the worst for His Son. As hard as the attack was for Job, Jesus' cup that He was about to drink (Matt. 20:22) intensely exceeded that of all others. Even beyond this, it would explain the immense differences between the events of the initial temptation early in the Gospels as contrasted with those during Satan's God-given hour of the darkness. Also, when Jesus warned Peter about Satan's attack on the Eleven, Jesus said nothing at that time about Satan making a request before God regarding Him and an hour of darkness, saving this revelation until His arrest. Satan may have gained permission to sift the eleven disciples like wheat, and God made an additional offer for Satan to consider. As with Job 1–2, God Himself may have been the initiator in this fulfillment of Satan's "beyond his wildest dreams:" other than death, full access to Jesus for one designated, divinely restricted hour of the darkness. This would explain many of Satan's activities during the days leading up to the crucifixion, including one more important activity that we will see in the next chapter.

Everything was different once Jesus was arrested and "the hour/authority of the darkness is yours" commenced in Luke 22:53. But why only then was everything different and not before? Why did Satan not do earlier at the first temptation of Jesus all that he would do in his hour of the darkness? The simple answer is that either God did not permit it, or that Satan may not ever have considered it as a possibility that the Godhead would permit it. So, careful contrasts can be made between the events of the crucifixion and those of Satan's initial tempting of Jesus years earlier. Jesus experienced hunger beyond the point that virtually any one else would experience with His forty day fast; however, nothing in the early temptation account speaks of Jesus as being in further agony. In the first temptation, there does not appear to have been any physical torturing of Jesus. Nothing is noted about His appearance having been being changed more than any man (Isa. 52:14). Nothing in the biblical account speaks of Satan actually touching God's Son. But that would soon change.

The grace of God would be magnified in that the consideration God placed before Satan would not have been limited only to Job. When people question, "How could God do such a thing to Job?" the more astounding question is "How could God do such a thing to His own Son?" And as we saw in *The Darkness and the Glory*, as horrible as the suffering was for Job, it was absolutely the ultimate of suffering for Jesus. God in His mercy would not allow Job to be tempted beyond what he was able (1 Cor. 10:13), but *no one* was able to go where Jesus went (John 13:33). At some time—and again, probably in the days leading up to Passover—Satan had to receive from God the "hour and the power/authority of the darkness" that he had not possessed earlier.

When considered this way, Luke 22 makes the early temptation by Satan in Luke 4 seem tremendously weaker in its intensity. By no means does one take away the suffering from the earlier temptation and how arduous it was for Jesus, but at that time He had not yet resolutely set His face like flint (Luke 9:51; Isa. 50:7) to go to Jerusalem to fully drink the Cup that the Father had given Him (John 18:11) which would include enduring the horrid hour of authority given to Satan and his entire assemblage (Luke 22:53)—plus much, much more.

Included within this account of Jesus' arrest, however, is one more important encounter with Satan. And unlike any of the previous ones, this episode is directly related to the face of God.

CHAPTER NINE

THE EYES

When Paul wrote Second Corinthians, he employed some of his harshest language ever recorded from him, especially in reference to the false apostles who were spiritually cannibalizing the less-than-godly Corinthian church:

> For such men are false apostles, deceitful workers, disguising themselves as apostles of Christ. And no wonder, for even Satan disguises himself as an angel of light. Therefore it is not surprising if his servants also disguise themselves as servants of righteousness; whose end shall be according to their deeds (2 Cor. 11:13–15).

Yet in the opening passage of this scathing section of the epistle (2 Cor. 10–13), Paul began in a rather surprising way with a statement associated not with strength but rather with meekness: "Now I, Paul, myself urge you by the meekness and gentleness of Christ [Messiah]—I who am meek when face to face with you, but bold toward you when absent!" (2 Cor. 10:1). Paul used a great deal of sarcasm in this section, which was fitting for the circumstances before him and the enemies of the Word that he was forced to denounce. But instead of listing his background or the apostolic authority granted to him by God, Paul urged the Corinthians by meekness and gentleness—not in reference to himself—but in reference to that of the Messiah.

"The meekness and gentleness of Messiah/Christ"—what a lovely thought to those who are saved and walking with our Lord; what utter folly to others who either do not know Him or do not currently obey Him. True biblical meekness is never equated with weakness; true meekness is always strength under control. The demons who approached Jesus throughout the Gospel accounts hardly viewed Him as meek; every encounter showed that they cowered whenever Jesus was in their midst or talked to them. Jesus still possessed authority even in His meekness, and the demons knew it exceedingly more than the earthly enemies knew it. Having once been part of the holy angels themselves before they fell, they had previously worshiped Him in heaven; now during His Incarnation (which they did not to any degree understand), they nonetheless always responded in fear and respect—always.

One of the best ways to show the vast difference between the worshipful adoration that Jesus received in heaven before His Incarnation and then His meekness during His earthly life is to contrast Philippians 2 with a passage we have seen before, Isaiah 6:1–5. Isaiah reveals aspects of what Jesus enjoyed before being born into meekness in Bethlehem:

> In the year of King Uzziah's death, I saw the Lord sitting on a throne, lofty and exalted, with the train of His robe filling the temple. Seraphim stood above Him, each having six wings; with two he covered his face, and with two he covered his feet, and with two he flew. And one called out to another and said, "Holy, Holy, Holy, is the LORD of hosts, the whole earth is full of His glory." And the foundations of the thresholds trembled at the voice of him who called out, while the temple was filling with smoke. Then I

said, "Woe is me, for I am ruined! Because I am a man of unclean lips, and I live among a people of unclean lips; for my eyes have seen the King, the LORD of hosts."

A simple summarized description of the Incarnation in Philippians 2:5–8, plus the command for us to have the same attitude that Jesus had, shows the incomparable contrast of what Jesus gave up when He left His heaven: "Have this attitude in yourselves which was also in Christ Jesus, who, although He existed in the form of God, did not regard equality with God a thing to be grasped, but emptied Himself, taking the form of a bond-servant, and being made in the likeness of men. And being found in appearance as a man, He humbled Himself by becoming obedient to the point of death, even death on a cross." When Jesus emptied Himself—at the point of the conception—He went from being in the presence of the other Godhead members, the seraphim and myriads of attending angels (Dan. 7:10), to be encased within the womb of a loving yet sinful woman of Adam's fallen, sinful lineage. In His High Priestly Prayer of John 17, just moments before Gethsemane, Jesus made reference to what He had once enjoyed and what He was ultimately returning to by praying, "Now, Father, glorify Me together with Yourself, with the glory which I had with You before the world was" (John 17:5). It is important to note that Philippians 2:5 states, "have this attitude in yourselves which *was* also in Christ Jesus"—not currently *is* in Christ Jesus. The stepping down meekness was a onetime only segment of Jesus' life. You can read Revelation 1, 19, and 20 to see some attributes and activities of the Word of God who will return to conquer and reclaim what is rightfully His and how greatly different this will be from the meekness of His first advent.

Isaiah 6 is the only place in Scripture that contains a reference to a special subset of angels known as seraphim, literally "burning ones" who stood above—and closely to—God. How many seraphim exist, God did not reveal. We are told that these beautiful, perfect creatures in Isaiah 6:2–3 had six wings consisting of two sets of three. Scholars have noted that they employ two-thirds of the wings that God had created for them in worship and one-third in service. They cover their faces—and this would include their eyes—before the Holy Presence of the Holy God. Unlike the prophet Isaiah, these are not sinful beings; they are not creatures of unclean lips—only holy. Nothing in the text indicates that the seraphim were commanded to cover their faces and their feet; they seem to do this naturally as a reverential act of worship freely and lovingly to the One who alone is worthy. Also, the covering of the face in worshipful adoration is not a universal designation of all angelic activity. Matthew 18:10 reveals that other angels of God specifically have a different task that they perform: "See that you do not despise one of these little ones, for I say to you, that their angels in heaven continually behold the face of My Father who is in heaven." One set of angels is not superior by beholding the face of the Father, and the others are not more holy or reverent by not doing so; they merely have different functions as they were so created by their Creator to perform (Col. 1:16).

It is intriguing to think how the seraphim would have viewed the Incarnation because, as we saw in a previous chapter, John 12:41 reveals this monumental truth about Isaiah 6: "These things Isaiah said because He saw His glory, and he spoke of Him." Did the seraphim continue to worship the remaining two members of the Godhead, or did they wait until the Ascension of Jesus to resume their worshipful activities? Did they uncover and turn their faces to witness the birth, life, death, and ascension of Jesus? We are not told this in Scripture, but it will be fascinating to find out when we get to heaven what they did for over thirty years because, as is true with all holy angels of God, they always desire to look into things that accompany salvation (1 Pet. 1:12).

So consider the ramifications of the holy Lamb of God, who took on flesh and dwelt among fallen man (John 1:14), "meek and gentle" (2 Cor. 10:1), when He encountered the utterly evil and violently wicked Satan during the forty-day temptation of Matthew 4/Mark 1/Luke 4. We should mark in our minds that the texts do not offer any description of the means by which Satan tempted Jesus. The Bible presents nothing about Satan appearing to Him: he may or may not have appeared; Jesus may have been able to see Satan without any special manifestation by the devil; we just do not know. But three differences in this temptation versus the other encounters that Jesus had with demons as recorded in later biblical passages dramatically stand out in contrast. First, unlike every other case whenever demons talked with Jesus, Satan used no human vehicle to communicate with Him, that is, no demon-possessed man was part of the temptation account. Second, every other biblical account has the fallen angels cowering in Jesus' presence; Satan did not. None of the dialogue recorded in these chapters gives any indication that Satan fearfully interacted with Him. Satan may very well have greatly feared Jesus—and for good reason—but he did not demonstrate this to the One Whom he tempted in the wilderness. Third, none of the other fallen angels ever tempted Jesus to sin; they only feared for their freedom in view of their impending judgment (Matt. 8:28–34; Mark 5:1–7; Luke 8:26–37). Satan actively plotted and tempted, and then when he failed in causing Jesus to stumble and, as we saw earlier, "he departed from Him until an opportune time" (Luke 4:13).

Later, as the days of Jesus' crucifixion drew near, in an expanded opportune time, Satan's approach to Jesus was still just as brazen as it had been in the wilderness temptation. Yet this time the brazenness of Satan went to a new unfathomable depth beyond that of any other time in the history of the world, as the evil one once more approached the Son of God who had emptied Himself of the free use of His Godhead authority.

♦ ♦ ♦ ♦ ♦ ♦ ♦

As we saw in the previous chapter of this book, many Bible readers know that Satan entered into Judas to help the human enemies of Jesus bring about the crucifixion. Luke 22:1–4 clearly shows this:

> Now the Feast of Unleavened Bread, which is called the Passover, was approaching. And the chief priests and the scribes were seeking how they might put Him to death; for they were afraid of the people. And Satan entered into Judas who was called Iscariot, belonging to the number of the twelve. And he went away and discussed with the chief priests and officers how he might betray Him to them.

Judas was not demon possessed; he was Satan possessed. The description "son of perdition/destruction" occurs only twice in the entire Bible: first, in reference to Judas (John 17:12) and later in reference to the future antichrist (2 Thess. 2:3). The exact Greek phrase is used to describe both people. If other instances exist of this full and unique indwelling by Satan, God does not reveal this in Scripture.

However, as we also saw in the previous chapter, what may be overlooked is that the Bible presents two different entrances of Satan into Judas—not one. John 13:26–27 records the second entrance: "Jesus therefore answered, 'That is the one for whom I shall dip the morsel and give it to him.' So when He had dipped the morsel, He took and gave it to Judas, the son of Simon Iscariot. And after the morsel, Satan then entered into him. Jesus therefore said to him, 'What you do, do quickly.'" In Luke 22 the Feast of Passover was approaching; in John 13 Jesus was eating His last Passover with His twelve apostles days after He had entered Jerusalem, and the subsequent events took place just a few hours before His arrest (Matt. 21:1–26:19). Therefore, the two entrances of Satan into Judas are days removed from each other. And if you have not already run ahead to the question, let me set it before you once more: *why did Satan enter Judas twice?* In John 13:27 it is evident that Satan had not yet entered into Judas, so the devil would have had to have departed from this wicked betrayer at some undisclosed point, and then after Judas ate the Passover element that Jesus handed him, Satan immediately entered into Judas' body for the second time.

Why two entrances of Satan into Judas? Would not one suffice?

In answering this, we should acknowledge that we would know nothing about either the Luke 22:3 or John 13:26–27 account unless God had revealed it, such is the nature of all behind the scenes spiritual truths. However, since God did put both of these episodes in His Word, it is evident that He wants us to know that these two entrances of Satan into Judas occurred. Sometimes we are even led to follow the trail and "connect the dots" to gain a better understanding of—and to marvel at—the sheer grace of God through the Lord Jesus Christ.

From the evidence given in Luke 22 and John 13, it reasons that the following scenario took place. Satan entered into Judas in order to bring about the events of the crucifixion and interact with the human enemies of Jesus (Luke 22:3–4) as the Feast of Unleavened Bread was approaching (Luke 22:1), that is, sometime very near to the final Passover week after Jesus had ridden into Jerusalem at the so-called "Triumphal Entry" (Luke 19:29–44) and clearly days before the cross. And as we have also previously seen, John 13:1–2 shows both Jesus' full awareness of what was about to occur as well as His great love for His own; but the text also discloses both Satan's preliminary activity and the spiritual condition of Judas' wicked heart:

> Now before the Feast of the Passover, Jesus knowing that His hour had come that He should depart out of this world to the Father, having loved His own who were in the world, He loved them to the end. And during supper, the devil having already put into the heart of Judas Iscariot, the son of Simon, to betray Him...

It is within this same context that the second entrance of Satan into Judas would soon occur (John 13:26–27). Since John's Gospel depicts the second entrance of Satan, obviously at some point Satan would have departed out of Judas after Luke 22:3 to go elsewhere. From evidence in Scripture, we know with absolute certainty that the devil went into the presence of God the Father in heaven and asked and was granted permission to sift the Eleven like wheat (Luke 22:31). It is important that Satan saw fit to exit from Judas and go somewhere else because it factors into our understanding of many related verses and helps us gain a better perspective: though Satan is powerful to a degree acknowledged by other high-ranking angels (Jude 9), nonetheless, he remains a created being. And as a created being, he is not omnipresent, which is an attribute of the Godhead only. Simply put, Satan cannot be personally present in two places at once. When he was inside Judas, he could not go before the Father in heaven; likewise, when he made his request before God to sift the disciples, he had to temporarily vacate Judas in order to make his request in heaven before the throne of God. And because what we saw in the previous chapter is true, it was during this same encounter that he made his request about the Eleven—which God granted—and most likely at this point received his unexpected hour of the authority of the darkness (Luke 22:53)—which God also granted. To state it another way, it is similar to Satan's coming away with more authority and status in the Garden after Adam and Eve sinned in Genesis 3 than he had when he first went there. Satan came away with more authority granted to him than he had expected when he left heaven to return to earth. We do not know the exact timeframe, but it is possible that his request about the Eleven and his unexpected receiving the hour of darkness may have been on the very day that Jesus would be betrayed. We will have to wait until God's full disclosure to His redeemed ones.

So now the final events of the night that Jesus was betrayed can be seen more clearly—as well as their utter importance—as they show Jesus having full knowledge of what was transpiring and what was about to happen to Him, and even more so, to show Him in a magnanimous display of grace upon grace of "having loved His own who were in the world, He loved them to the end" (John 13:1).

♦ ♦ ♦ ♦ ♦ ♦

Years ago a popular movie on the passion of Christ presented Satan tempting Jesus in the Garden of Gethsemane (I have been told this; I chose not to see the movie). Others have either written about Satan tempting Jesus in Gethsemane or have portrayed this idea through some visual media such as paintings. But that is clearly a biblical impossibility: Satan cannot reside inside of Judas as he walked to arrest Jesus and be at Gethsemane at the same time. As we have seen, although he is powerful, Satan cannot be two places at the same time.

So consider then some of the biblical significance of the two different entrances of Satan into Judas. After all, it is one thing to know that something happened; it is another thing to understand some of its theological importance to behold the total sovereignty and authority of the Lamb of God. As we have previously seen, the account of John 13:24–27 describes the setting for the second entrance into Judas:

> Simon Peter therefore gestured to him, and said to him, "Tell us who it is of whom He is speaking." He,

leaning back thus on Jesus' breast, said to Him, "Lord, who is it?"

Jesus therefore answered, "That is the one for whom I shall dip the morsel and give it to him." So when He had dipped the morsel, He took and gave it to Judas, the son of Simon Iscariot. And after the morsel, Satan then entered into him. Jesus therefore said to him, "What you do, do quickly."

Once John 13:27 took place and Satan again entered Judas at the Passover meal, Jesus stared not only into the eyes of Judas—Jesus stared into the eyes of Satan. If God saw fit, this may have been the first time that Satan actually got to stare into the eyes of Jesus during the Incarnation, or at least to get this close.

"What you do, do quickly" (John 13:27). Jesus commanded and dismissed Judas; Jesus commanded and dismissed Satan. So after receiving the morsel, when Judas went out (John 13:30), Satan went out. With the two enemies of Jesus no longer present, the Savior could begin teaching His beloved disciples these deep, deep theological truths until the time of His arrest in John 18. The verse following Judas' departure reads: "When therefore he [Judas, but also Satan] had gone out, Jesus said, 'Now is the Son of Man glorified, and God is glorified in Him'" (John 13:31). Of course, the Eleven were protectively oblivious to what was taking place. All they would have seen was Judas leaving. They would not know about Satan's role until after the Resurrection. The angelic world who was watching—both holy and demonic—would have seen these things and likely would have marveled at why Jesus would have allowed Satan's intensified role.

After the somber Passover, when Jesus left the upper room, He took His eleven disciples to a quiet place that would not stay quiet for long: "When Jesus had spoken these words, He went forth with His disciples over the ravine of Kidron, where there was a garden

[Gethsemane], into which He Himself entered, and His disciples" (John 18:1). Among Jesus' cries of "Abba! Father!" followed by the trampling of the assemblage who arrested Him, this peaceful garden would temporarily have its peace disrupted.

John 18:1 states that Jesus went to Gethsemane with His disciples, which, of course, meant all who were with Him at the Passover meal except Judas. So it is fitting that when John recorded the arrest of Jesus, three different times he specifically lists Judas by name as being at the place of arrest. John 18:2: "Now Judas also, who was betraying Him, knew the place; for Jesus had often met there with His disciples." Again in John 18:3: "Judas then, having received the Roman cohort, and officers from the chief priests and the Pharisees, came there with lanterns and torches and weapons." And in the absolute real sense, when Judas came to the Garden to arrest Jesus, Satan also came there inside this wicked one who had never truly been saved.

But there is one more important instance. John 18:4 reveals, "Jesus therefore, knowing all the things that were coming upon Him, went forth, and said to them, 'Whom do you seek?'" John 18:5 gives the answer and notes for the third time who is there: "They answered Him, 'Jesus the Nazarene.' He said to them, 'I am He.' And Judas also who was betraying Him, was standing with them"—but not for long. As Judas was standing there, Satan was standing inside him. How appropriately John 18:6 unveils, "When therefore He said to them, 'I am He,' they drew back, and fell to the ground." Jesus employed the name "I AM/Yahweh," (*ego eimi* in the Greek text); the "He" is usually italicized in the English translations to make it read smoother; literally it reads, "I am" not "I am He." So in a most restricted preview of Philippian 2:9–11: "Therefore also God highly exalted Him, and bestowed on Him the name which is above every name, *that at the name of Jesus* every knee should bow, of those who are in heaven, and on earth, and under the earth, and that every tongue should confess that Jesus Christ is Lord, to the glory of God the Father." The entire multitude drew back and fell to the ground before they realized what had happened—and that included Judas—and that included Satan. Foolish, non-Bible believing scholars have written that Jesus had gotten in over His head at this final Passover, that He never intended to be crucified, and that events ran away from Him so that He had no choice from this point onward. However, from John's account alone, does any doubt exist about who remained in sovereign control in every aspect of His arrest? Putting the arresting band of Roman soldiers and Jewish temple guards temporarily on the ground was no great work for this One who will one day speak the resurrection and judgment into existence:

> "Truly, truly, I say to you, an hour is coming and now is, when the dead shall hear the voice of the Son of God; and those who hear shall live. For just as the Father has life in Himself, even so He gave to the Son also to have life in Himself; and He gave Him authority to execute judgment, because He is the Son of Man. Do not marvel at this; for an hour is coming, in which all who are in the tombs shall hear His voice, and shall come forth; those who did the good deeds to a resurrection of life, those who committed the evil deeds to a resurrection of judgment" (John 5:25–29).

He could have spoken them all at the time into their eternal destinies—including Satan (Matt. 25:41)—if such had been His desire and purpose. But it was not; the One who had set His face like flint had much to accomplish to redeem and restore—and to crush forever the head of the serpent of old, Satan the devil (Rev. 12:9).

Yet one more item to note occurs as the arrest followed shortly thereafter. Matthew 26:47–50, Mark 14:43–45, and Luke 22:47–53 all record the account with which we are so familiar: Judas betraying

Jesus with a kiss or kisses. And as we have seen before, when Judas approached and kissed Jesus, Satan approached and kissed Jesus. Of course, nobody present other than those of the holy world and those of the demonic world would have known that a much deeper spiritual encounter was taking place; those present saw only the physical participants.

The demons watching would have observed their tyrannous dictator approach and then do something unheard for them, *never* would the thought have crossed the minds of demons to kiss the Son of God on His holy face. Go through the Gospel accounts if you like and see if you can find a trace that the demons considered kissing Jesus during their encounters with Him. *Never* would it have crossed the holy angels' minds (unless God had revealed to them what was taking place) that God the Father would ever permit such degradation of His only beloved Son. What Satan anticipated in this brazen, previously unallowed encounter, we do not know. If Satan expected Jesus to respond in revulsion, he erred eternally; Jesus responded in grace and submission to the Father's will to drink the Cup that the Father had given Him. And when Jesus then gave the announcement, "but this hour, and the power of the darkness are yours" (Luke 22:53), *no one* would have understood the explanation better than Satan. If Satan had any doubts about whether or not Jesus knew what God the Father had granted him, they were now removed. Jesus knew, yet Jesus submitted. The hour of Satan's authority had begun in Gethsemane with the kiss, and every second moved that hour closer and closer to its termination.

Consider then some of the cascading ramifications of what we have seen.

Sinlessly perfect Seraphim, holy and pure, cover their faces in the presence of pre-incarnate Jesus, and this obviously would include their eyes (Isa. 6:2). Yet Jesus did not regard equality with God a thing to be grasped but emptied Himself into the fallen world He Himself had once created as holy (Phil. 2:5–8), temporarily setting aside this worshipful adoration.

Holy seraphim cover their faces in the presence of God; yet Mary and Joseph—recipients of Adam's fall and the resulting curse—look into the face—and ultimately into the eyes—of their newly born Son who was in no way affected by Adam's fall. Mary and Joseph looked into the face of God Incarnate, and they did so every day that they talked with Jesus, yet they did this by God's grace, God's design and God's love—and with God's great joy and delight. And each day they received the blessing that God will ultimately give to the Jewish nation—and ultimately anyone else—once they have repented and have been restored to true New Covenant relationship and obedience to Yahweh: the LORD did bless and keep Mary and Joseph; the LORD did make His face to shine on them and was gracious unto them; the LORD did lift up His face on them and give them peace.

Holy seraphim cover their faces in the presence of God; demons did so during the meekness of Jesus during the Incarnation. How much more would the demons do so now after Jesus was taken up in glory (1 Tim. 3:16) shuddering at the thought of His return to capture, judge and cast them into the lake of fire originally prepared for them and their leader, whom they so foolishly followed (Jam. 2:19; Matt. 25:41).

Holy seraphim cover their faces in the presence of God; Satan did not cover his face. However, everything about Satan's status changed when Jesus cried, "It is finished." Never again will Satan have the hour of the darkness; never again will he touch Jesus. In all probability, he cannot make eye contact with the holy eyes of Jesus (Rev. 1:14) even when God summons him—if God still summons him—until Satan will ultimately be cast out of heaven in the fast-approaching Tribulation (Rev. 12:7–9) and shortly thereafter ultimately—and eternally—cast into hell itself (Rev. 20:10).

Holy seraphim cover their faces in the presence of God; Judas and the other eternally damned will cover their faces at the Great White Throne Judgment of Revelation 20.

Jesus secured every one of these truths during His meekness and gentleness. How much more then will take place when He returns and the full Glory of God?

CHAPTER TEN

THE GLORY

"Then God said, 'Let there be light;' and there was light."

While this beautiful, simple statement of divine cause and effect also records the first command that God ever gave in Scripture, this fiat pronouncement is part of a larger segment of God's creative order:

> In the beginning God created the heavens and the earth. And the earth was formless and void, and darkness was over the surface of the deep; and the Spirit of God was moving over the surface of the waters. Then God said, "Let there be light"; and there was light. And God saw that the light was good; and God separated the light from the darkness. And God called the light day, and the darkness He called night. And there was evening and there was morning, one day (Gen. 1:1–5).

For those who love God and His Word, this is the divine explanation that He gives as not only what happened, but more importantly, Who made it happen. For those who love neither God nor His Word, this is still the divine explanation that God gives—He offers no other. Reception or rejection of His truth never diminishes what is true; it only concerns the relationship or lack thereof to both God and His Word. This description of God and His creation carries much greater importance than many people realize. Contrary to what those who skeptically read the Bible claim, "It really does not matter how one interprets Genesis 1–2," it actually does matter immensely. How one interprets—or misinterprets—Genesis 1–2 locks one into how he or she approaches the remainder of the Bible.

Harsh critics of the Bible love to take Genesis 1–2 and ridicule anyone who would accept this as anything more than mythical fiction. But although they usually consider themselves on the cutting edge in bringing about new attacks concerning the truthfulness of God and His Word, they are actually doing nothing new. In fact, they currently stand in a long line of doubters of God's Word, and most of them are affected by the spiritual condition of the unredeemed that they would never consider true about themselves, nor would they acknowledge that such a spiritual condition even existed.

"Then God said" occurs nine times in Genesis 1. In Genesis 2:16, God took His newly created son Adam and "commanded, saying"—which is the first command to humanity recorded in Scripture and the tenth time stated that God said something. By contrast, the first question recorded in the Bible is by an enemy of the Truth, who, in spite of the multiple "Then God said" statements, this unannounced, fallen being asks an at-that-time unfallen creature, "Indeed has God said?" (Gen. 3:1). This simple question of doubting if God had said what He had said and had actually meant it, without the proper response by the second created being, worked its utter devastation with Eve, who in turn ensnared Adam in her sin—and sinfulness. Tragically, the same question and stumbling block has ensnared millions of individuals, churches, denominations, and seminaries from Genesis 3 to the present day. This simple question by the enemy worked perfectly when asked to a holy creature in a perfect environment with no effects of sin at that time, only beauty and holiness; how much more effective then is this same accusatory question of doubt when asked to fallen man in the midst of "a crooked and perverse generation" (Phil. 2:15)?

Those who deny the truthfulness of God's Word are affected in varying degrees by the same enemy who attacked Adam and Eve, although, as is the case throughout the Bible and later in church history, they would never acknowledge or consider an enemy's influence in their own lives. If they are unsaved, Second Corinthians 4:3–4 plainly explains what their spiritual condition currently is and who actively works to maintain their blind condition: "And even if our gospel is veiled, it is veiled *to those who are perishing*, in whose case the god of this world *has blinded the minds of the unbelieving*, that they might not see the light of the gospel of the glory of Christ, who is the image of God." "Those who are perishing," and "the unbelieving" best characterize those who are currently alive but unsaved. Two quick points to note: first, if they are not saved and they ultimately perish, the veiling of the Gospel ends for them at the moment of their death, as they awaken in torture in Hades awaiting the final judgment of Revelation 20. Second, Satan actively "blinds the minds of the unbelieving," which is the arena of battle for him from Genesis 3 to Revelation 20. He does not have to blind an unsaved heart; it responds naturally against God by its very existence. (Eph. 2:1–3; 4:17–19).

Ephesians 2:1–3 delineates these characteristics of the lost which would have included us before we received salvation:

> And you were dead in your trespasses and sins, in which you formerly walked according to the course of this world, according to the prince of the power of the air, of the spirit that is now working in the sons of disobedience. Among them we too all formerly lived in the lusts of our flesh, indulging the desires of the flesh and of the mind, and were by nature children of wrath, even as the rest.

Ephesians 4:17–19 adds this description of all of those spiritually lost:

> This I say therefore, and affirm together with the Lord, that you walk no longer just as the [unsaved] Gentiles also walk, in the futility of their mind, being darkened in their understanding, excluded from the life of God, because of the ignorance that is in them, because of the hardness of their heart; and they, having become callous, have given themselves over to sensuality, for the practice of every kind of impurity with greediness.

First Timothy 4:1–2 discloses the demonic realm's active work in continuously disseminating false doctrine: "But the Spirit explicitly says that in later times some will fall away from the faith, paying attention to deceitful spirits and doctrines of demons, by means of the hypocrisy of liars seared in their own conscience as with a branding iron." That "deceitful spirits" even exist would be absurd to those who do not believe the Bible; that "doctrines of demons" are actively taught—especially in some seminaries and pulpits—would likewise be considered impossible by the skeptics. Nonetheless, God's standard of sound words remains, and what many consider as folly, God presents as treasure:

> Retain the standard of sound words which you have heard from me, in the faith and love which are in Christ Jesus. Guard, through the Holy Spirit who dwells in us, the treasure which has been entrusted to you (2 Tim. 1:13–14).

Interestingly, God discloses that doctrines of demons most assuredly exist, but He gives no information for what is or is not such demonic teachings. Because of this lack of disclosure, it should force lovers of God's Word to study the Bible to make every effort to handle the word of truth accurately (2 Tim. 2:15), very much believing that anyone who teaches God's Word will be held to a much stricter judgment by God (Jam. 3:1).

Among other things about the Genesis 1 account that critics of the Bible find laughable and love to ridicule is the order of creation. On the third day God created all vegetation (Gen. 1:9–13), but it is not until the fourth day that God created the sun, moon and stars (Gen. 1:14–19). What folly to think that vegetation could exist before the sun existed, they argue, and this presents to them what seems to be an insurmountable problem for accepting the veracity of the Genesis account. Two options are possible to explain this perceived enigma: "Well, I never thought of that," God later lamented to Himself (terrible, *terrible* theology).

Or ... God used another source of Light.

✦ ✦ ✦ ✦ ✦ ✦

Multiple accounts exist throughout Scripture that contrast the eternal with the temporal. Everything about the attributes of God is eternal; everything about angels and demons is eternal; everything about heaven and hell is eternal; and everything about the human soul is eternal for both the saved and the lost. For the inanimate part of God's creation, however, it is an entirely different story. When Jesus said in Matthew 24:35: "Heaven and earth will pass away, but My words shall not pass away," He contrasted the eternal capacity of His truth with the certain demise of the heavens and the earth that God created in Genesis 1. We should not overlook this tremendously important doctrinal truth: the eternal existed long before and will exist long after the temporary has completely passed away.

The study of the eternality of God and His Word is far too broad a subject for this book, so we will focus briefly on a sampling of the transitory nature of the heavens and the earth. In Isaiah 24, God reveals this future condition of the earth that He created: "The earth will be completely laid waste and completely despoiled, for the LORD has spoken this word. The earth mourns and withers, the world fades and withers, the exalted of the people of the earth fade away (Isa. 24:3–4). Isaiah 24:19–20 further states, "The earth is broken asunder, the earth is split through, the earth is shaken violently. The earth reels to and fro like a drunkard, and it totters like a shack, for its transgression is heavy upon it, and it will fall, never to rise again." God explains that the fulfillment of these prophecies will occur with the return of the LORD:

> So it will happen in that day, that the LORD will punish the host of heaven, on high, and the kings of the earth, on earth. And they will be gathered together like prisoners in the dungeon, and will be confined in prison; and after many days they will be punished. Then the moon will be abashed and the sun ashamed, for the LORD of hosts will reign on Mount Zion and in Jerusalem, and His glory will be before His elders (Isa. 24:21–23).

Jesus followed suit in Matthew 24:29–31, teaching virtually the same thing but adding additional details:

> "But immediately after the tribulation of those days the sun will be darkened, and the moon will not give its light, and the stars will fall from the sky, and the powers of the heavens will be shaken, and then the sign of the Son of Man will appear in the sky, and then all the tribes of the earth will mourn, and they will see the Son of Man coming on the clouds of the sky with power and great glory. And He will send forth His angels with a great trumpet and they

will gather together His elect from the four winds, from one end of the sky to the other."

But if the Lord returns after the sun is destroyed in the Millennial Kingdom, how then will there be light? Isaiah 4:2–6 reveals part of this answer:

> In that day the Branch of the LORD will be beautiful and glorious, and the fruit of the earth will be the pride and the adornment of the survivors of Israel. And it will come about that he who is left in Zion and remains in Jerusalem will be called holy—everyone who is recorded for life in Jerusalem. When the Lord has washed away the filth of the daughters of Zion, and purged the bloodshed of Jerusalem from her midst, by the spirit of judgment and the spirit of burning, then the LORD will create over the whole area of Mount Zion and over her assemblies a cloud by day, even smoke, and the brightness of a flaming fire by night; for over all the glory will be a canopy. And there will be a shelter to give shade from the heat by day, and refuge and protection from the storm and the rain.

Isaiah 4:5 summarizes it best ("for over all the glory [of the LORD] will be a canopy") in language strikingly similar to that which was used when God first filled His Tabernacle with His own glory:

> Then the cloud covered the tent of meeting, and the glory of the LORD filled the tabernacle. And Moses was not able to enter the tent of meeting because the cloud had settled on it, and the glory of the LORD filled the tabernacle.
>
> And throughout all their journeys whenever the cloud was taken up from over the tabernacle, the sons of Israel

would set out; but if the cloud was not taken up, then they did not set out until the day when it was taken up. For throughout all their journeys, the cloud of the LORD was on the tabernacle by day, and there was fire in it by night, in the sight of all the house of Israel (Exod. 40:34–38).

Having a manifestation of the Glory of God show forth during the wilderness generation did not take away the sun's usefulness, although God certainly could have taken it away if He had desired to do that.

It is obvious that with the advent of the King and His Kingdom, the sun, moon, and stars will be returned to their celestial places because they must be present at the final judgment. Second Peter 3:10–13 prophesies of this coming end—and a new beginning:

> But the day of the Lord will come like a thief, in which the heavens will pass away with a roar and the elements will be destroyed with intense heat, and the earth and its works will be burned up. Since all these things are to be destroyed in this way, what sort of people ought you to be in holy conduct and godliness, looking for and hastening the coming of the day of God, on account of which the heavens will be destroyed by burning, and the elements will melt with intense heat! But according to His promise we are looking for new heavens and a new earth, in which righteousness dwells.

Revelation 20:11 explains that the prophecies of the destruction of the heavens and earth will be fully accomplished at the Great White Throne Judgment of the eternally damned: "And I saw a great white throne and Him who sat upon it, from whose presence earth and heaven fled away, and no place was found for them."

So the heavens and the earth will be destroyed, but then what?

♦ ♦ ♦ ♦ ♦ ♦

Of all the designations used for Jesus throughout Scripture, one is repeatedly used that is often noted in songs and in some books, but it is not the normal designation that many use for Jesus: "the Lamb of God," or simply just "The Lamb." Usually the title "Christ" or "Messiah" occurs. This is not wrong; it merely emphasizes a different function and capacity of Jesus.

The first instance of "the lamb" is fittingly used in Genesis 22:7–8 in a conversation between Abraham and Isaac while they were on Moriah:

> And Isaac spoke to Abraham his father and said, "My father!" And he said, "Here I am, my son." And he said, "Behold, the fire and the wood, but where is the lamb for the burnt offering?" And Abraham said, "God will provide for Himself the lamb for the burnt offering, my son." So the two of them walked on together.

(For those who want a much deeper study in this intensely rich section of Scripture, see "The Place" in *The Stone and the Glory*). The second reference to "the lamb" is just as fitting as the first, as God gave instructions regarding His Passover and the lambs that were to be used (Ex. 12:1–4) as He was about to redeem Israel out of Egypt—just as He had previously promised (Gen. 15:12–16; Exod. 2:24-25; 3:1–8).

The first two accounts of "the Lamb" reference in the New Testament are both made by John the Baptist in John 1: "The next day he saw Jesus coming to him, and said, 'Behold, the Lamb of God who takes away the sin of the world!'" (John 1:29). This is the first time the full use of "the Lamb of God" is used to describe Jesus. Later, John the Baptist said again in reference to Jesus to two of his disciples, "Behold the Lamb of God!" (John 1:36). One of the two disciples who heard John speak was later revealed to be Andrew, the brother of Simon Peter, who found his brother and brought Him to Jesus (John 1:40–42).

After this theologically loaded section which occurred in this very early ministry of Jesus, something rather unexpected occurs: the designation "the Lamb" does not occur again in the Bible until the Book of Revelation. As may be expected, "Christ" or "Messiah" is used instead, occurring 531 times from Matthew through Revelation. But once we get to Revelation, "Christ/Messiah" is used only 7 times; "the Lamb"—which after John 1 always describes the Lamb of God—occurs, that is 25 times in the Book of Revelation, almost four times more than the use of "Christ/Messiah."

Revelation 1:1, 2 and 5 use the term "Jesus Christ" in the opening verses of this prophecy, which by itself is almost one-half of all the uses of "Christ" in Revelation. Revelation 11:15 promises, "And the seventh angel sounded; and there arose loud voices in heaven, saying, 'The kingdom of the world has become the kingdom of our Lord, and of His Christ [Messiah]; and He will reign forever and ever.'" After a great war in heaven will one day occur, and after Satan and his demons will be cast to earth, the following reactive declaration is made: "And I heard a loud voice in heaven, saying, 'Now the salvation, and the power, and the kingdom of our God and the authority of His Christ have come, for the accuser of our brethren has been thrown down, who accuses them before our God day and night'" (Rev. 12:10). Fittingly, these two references in the middle of the Book of Revelation connect Messiah's Kingdom and His promised reign. It should not be surprising to find that the last two uses of Christ/Messiah in the Bible are found in Revelation 20 when the Kingdom reign occurs. Revelation 20:4 describes the following: "And

I saw thrones, and they sat upon them, and judgment was given to them. And I saw the souls of those who had been beheaded because of the testimony of Jesus and because of the word of God, and those who had not worshiped the beast or his image, and had not received the mark upon their forehead and upon their hand; and they came to life and reigned with Christ for a thousand years." Two verses later, the last usage in the Bible of Christ/Messiah occurs in Revelation 20:6: "Blessed and holy is the one who has a part in the first resurrection; over these the second death has no power, but they will be priests of God and of Christ and will reign with Him for a thousand years."

It is fitting that in Revelation 20, where the Kingdom reign is described, the last two uses of the word "Christ" occur, because as important as the fullness of the Kingdom will be, it does have a termination point, as 1 Corinthians 15:20–26 shows:

> But now Christ has been raised from the dead, the first fruits of those who are asleep. For since by a man came death, by a man also came the resurrection of the dead. For as in Adam all die, so also in Christ all shall be made alive. But each in his own order: Christ the first fruits, after that those who are Christ's at His coming, then comes the end, when He delivers up the kingdom to the God and Father, when He has abolished all rule and all authority and power. For He must reign until He has put all His enemies under His feet [note the Psalm 110:1 reference]. The last enemy that will be abolished is death. For He must reign until He has put all things in subjection under His feet.

Appropriately, the word "Christ" occurs four times in this section on the Kingdom and its ultimate fulfillment and termination. After all the events of Revelation 20, which includes the final earthly rebellion and the Great White Throne Judgment, something will exist with which we presently have no experiential knowledge: the complete absence of any sin, any effects of the curse, or any evil. The Kingdom will be delivered up to the Father (1 Cor. 15:24); the Son will have accomplished all judgment (John 5:22), including passing judgment on the eternally damned humans and on Satan and his demons; no adversaries will exist outside of the lake of fire. God will then have the free fellowship with His redeemed and will be accompanied by His myriads of myriads of holy angels (Rev. 5:11), all in perfect and complete fellowship—and joy (John 17:13)—as we behold His glory:

> "Father, I desire that they also, whom You have given Me, be with Me where I am, in order that they may behold My glory, which You have given Me; for You did love Me before the foundation of the world" (John 17:24).

After John the Baptist's "Behold the Lamb of God" statement in John 1:36, this precious title for God's Messiah does not occur again until the Book of Revelation, where it is used frequently. For instance, the designation "the Lamb" occurs nineteen times in Revelation 1–19, such as in Revelation 19:7: "Let us rejoice and be glad and give the glory to Him, for the marriage of the Lamb has come and His bride has made herself ready." This wonderful union will be followed by the eternally blissful description, "Blessed are those who are invited to the marriage supper of the Lamb" (Rev. 19:9). As we saw, the last two references of Christ/Messiah occur in Revelation 20, but "the Lamb" does not occur in this section. And then in the new heaven and the new earth—and with the advent of the New Jerusalem—Jesus takes on His eternal designation by which He has chosen to be called—the Lamb. This blessed, sweet title and description of Him occurs six times in Revelation 21–22, and it explains Who He is, some of what He has done, and what He will accomplish.

The opening verses of Revelation 21 reveal the first disclosure of our future home—and even more important—our future indescribable relationship:

> And I saw a new heaven and a new earth; for the first heaven and the first earth passed away, and there is no longer any sea. And I saw the holy city, new Jerusalem, coming down out of heaven from God, made ready as a bride adorned for her husband. And I heard a loud voice from the throne, saying, "Behold, the tabernacle of God is among men, and He shall dwell among them, and they shall be His people, and God Himself shall be among them, and He shall wipe away every tear from their eyes; and there shall no longer be any death; there shall no longer be any mourning, or crying, or pain; the first things have passed away (Rev. 21:1–4).

It is within this context that the first reference to the Lamb occurs as God's perfect holy city will descend from the heavens in Revelation 21:9–11:

> And one of the seven angels who had the seven bowls full of the seven last plagues, came and spoke with me, saying, "Come here, I shall show you the bride, the wife of the Lamb." And he carried me away in the Spirit to a great and high mountain, and showed me the holy city, Jerusalem, coming down out of heaven from God, having the glory of God. Her brilliance was like a very costly stone, as a stone of crystal-clear jasper.

The description "having the glory of God" (Rev. 21:11) cannot be overstated in its importance, as the Glory of God will be one of the things that makes heaven truly be heaven. Note also, in

Revelation 21:14, instead of receiving the designation "the apostles of Christ/Messiah," they then will be called "the twelve apostles of the Lamb."

The breathtaking description of Revelation 21:22–23 reveals and explains those things that will neither be present nor needed in the eternal state: "And I saw no temple in it, for the Lord God, the Almighty, and the Lamb, are its temple. And the city has no need of the sun or of the moon to shine upon it, for the glory of God has illumined it, and its lamp is the Lamb." The final two uses of the Lamb of God add additional blessings of God:

> And he showed me a river of the water of life, clear as crystal, coming from the throne of God and of the Lamb, in the middle of its street. And on either side of the river was the tree of life, bearing twelve kinds of fruit, yielding its fruit every month; and the leaves of the tree were for the healing of the nations. And there shall no longer be any curse; and the throne of God and of the Lamb shall be in it, and His bond-servants shall serve Him (Rev. 22:1–3).

Also, then the full disclosure that at one time was limited and restricted (1 Pet. 1:8) will no longer be so: "and they shall see His face, and His name shall be on their foreheads" (Rev. 22:4). Again we have the blessed reminder of God's every provision for those who are rightly related to Him in perfect union throughout eternity: "And there shall no longer be any night; and they shall not have need of the light of a lamp nor the light of the sun, because the Lord God shall illumine them; and they shall reign forever and ever" (Rev. 22:5).

Every aspect of the blessing of God in Numbers 6 will be present and operative, then will be multiplied billions and billions of times over in the eternal state for all of the eternally redeemed, both Jew and Gentile. The LORD will bless us and keep us; the LORD will make

His face—which we shall see—shine upon us as the dispersing lamp of the Glory of God, and He will already have been gracious to us because while the Lamb is a blessed name for the One in our midst, it is also an eternal reminder that it was the Lamb who took away our sin so that we could have life eternal (John 1:29). The LORD will lift up His face on us, and give His redeemed ones eternal, uninterrupted peace—and joy—in a resurrected body specifically designed to enjoy the presence of God and all the currently unrevealed treasures that accompany that eternal relationship with Him.

That New Jerusalem will have no need for the sun or the moon because the glory of God has illumined it, and that the holy vessel by which this glory will be dispersed throughout all of God's creations (except hell, 2 Thess. 1:9) will be the Lamb. Revelation 21:23 fits the divine disclosure that is given of Jesus given in Hebrews 1:3 that He is "the radiance of His glory." Jesus as the Second Member of the Godhead is the means by which all aspects of God's glory show forth. This will be true into eternity future—and will never have an end.

But one more account pulls everything together and explains the creation order that God had performed in Genesis 1, although most critics of God and His Word will never accept this answer in their more restricted and limited lifetime.

♦ ♦ ♦ ♦ ♦ ♦ ♦

We saw Satan's current work in the minds of unbelievers in Second Corinthians 4:3–4: "And even if our gospel is veiled, it is veiled to those who are perishing, in whose case the god of this world has blinded the minds of the unbelieving, that they might not see the light of the gospel of the glory of Christ, who is the image of God." The next two verses that follow, Second Corinthians 4:5–6, show God's part in rescuing someone out of this spiritual death condition and also give the incredible revelation that we have nowhere else in

Scripture: "For we do not preach ourselves but Christ Jesus as Lord, and ourselves as your bond-servants for Jesus' sake. For God, who said, 'Light shall shine out of darkness,' is the One who has shone in our hearts to give the light of the knowledge of the glory of God in the face of Christ."

Second Corinthians 4:6 is the most sweeping, all-encompassing verse in the entire Bible, as it begins in Genesis 1, contains the salvation experience of Paul and the saved Corinthians (and anyone else who will be saved), which then leads to the glory of God, which ultimately takes it to Revelation 21–22 throughout all eternity. However, as we have seen, "Light shall shine out of darkness" in Genesis 1:3 is a reference to the Light of God in Day One of creation—*not* a reference to the sun being created for light on Day Four in Genesis 1:14–19. Neither God nor Paul made reference to the creation of the sun to illumine the world; they both refer to the manifestation of a different Light. So actually, Second Corinthians 4:6 contains two references to the Glory of God: one by description ("Let there be light") and the other by written designation ("the glory of God in the face of Christ/Messiah"). In a sense, the Glory of God not only "bookends" this verse, the Glory of God "bookends" the entire Bible beginning in Genesis 1 and used lastly—and throughout all eternity—forever in the eternal state as shown in Revelation 21–22.

The God who will one day eternally illumine His creation by means of the Glory of God through the lamp of the Lamb of God (Rev. 21:23), so that there will be no need for the sun or the moon, had previously done the same thing in a temporary fashion before He created the sun, moon, or stars in Genesis 1. And while John would later be inspired by the Holy Spirit to write more in reference to the Lamb of God throughout the Book of Revelation, Paul understood the truth of Hebrews 1:3 that Jesus "is the radiance of His glory" whether or not this verse had been penned by that time Hebrews was written. God choose to radiate His glory "in the face of Christ" (2 Cor. 4:6), and did so not only at the Transfiguration as a preview of what was to come, but also as part of the creation account of His creation.

"Whose Son is the Messiah?" (Matt. 22:42).

Jesus is much, much more than only the Son of David. God illumined a darkened world through the face of His Messiah before there were any plants, animals—or humans created in the image of God and did so long before His own birth in humble Bethlehem. And indeed "God saw that the Light was good" (Gen. 1:4)

One closing thought: the last words of Jesus recorded in Scripture are, "Yes, I am coming quickly" (Rev. 22:20). Obviously, this statement makes sense to us as the Book of Revelation ends, and the exhortation and reminder of His return—and reward: "Behold, I am coming quickly, and My reward is with Me, to render to every man according to what he has done" (Rev. 22:12). These and other such verses should motivate us to live godly and to be about the Master's work until He returns, or until we as individuals go home to be with Him at our death, as instructed in 2 Corinthians 5:6–9:

> Therefore, being always of good courage, and knowing that while we are at home in the body we are absent from the Lord—for we walk by faith, not by sight—we are of good courage, I say, and prefer rather to be absent from the body and to be at home with the Lord. Therefore also we have as our ambition, whether at home or absent, to be pleasing to Him.

But the next-to-the-last words of Jesus are often not noted: "I, Jesus, have sent My angel to testify to you these things for the churches. I am the root and the offspring of David, the bright morning star" (Rev. 22:16). Now why would Jesus want the churches to know that He is "the root and the offspring of David?" What is the significance of this declaration?

Among other things, including that many of the churches neglect the eternally important Davidic Covenant and its promises, Revelation 22:16 is the exact teaching that Jesus used when He questioned the Pharisees in Matthew 22:41–46 where He asked them, "What do you think about the Christ/Messiah, whose son is He?" To critics who have rejected Him or who currently reject Him, to those who have loved Him in the past, to those who currently love Him, and to those who will love Him in the future, Jesus firmly draws this dividing line in the sand: "I am the root of David—his lineage and dynasty originates from Me because I was David's Lord before I was born." "I am the offspring of David"—who did not regard equality with God a thing to be grasped but emptied Himself by becoming flesh to be born into the royal lineage.

"Whose son is the Messiah?"

The Son of David by human birth and genealogy; the Son of God beforehand and afterward—*and* the One on whom God radiated—and radiates—His Glory in Genesis 1 on the face of His Christ/Messiah" into eternity, with the Glory of God on the Face of Christ (2 Cor. 4:6), and He—Jesus alone—radiates the glory of God: "And He is the radiance of His glory and the exact representation of His nature, and upholds all things by the word of His power" (Heb. 1:3).

Still beyond all that we have seen, God grants us a divine sneak preview of what awaits His redeemed, and He does so in the most intimate way.

♦ ♦ ♦ ♦ ♦ ♦ ♦

Genesis 3 tragically ends with God's expulsion of His once holy children away from His presence. Sin kills; it always kills—sin separates; it always separates. Genesis 3:24 reveals that God stationed warrior cherubim angels to guard access to the tree of life—and to a large degree—access to Himself. Many years later, when God brought the nation of Israel into an additional covenant relationship with Him by ratifying the Mosaic Covenant (Ex. 24:1-8), God then revealed something completely different, and for the first time since Genesis 3, a partial reversal of His previous separation: "And let them construct a sanctuary for Me, that I may dwell among them. According to all that I am going to show you, as the pattern of the tabernacle and the pattern of all its furniture, just so you shall construct it" (Ex. 25:8-9). It is important to note that God had a specific pattern of how He wanted His Tabernacle erected; nothing about this was freelance or haphazardly thrown together.

From the instructions given in Exodus 27 and elsewhere, we know that the Tabernacle was a rectangular tent 100 cubits by 50 cubits, and with a cubit being 18 inches (or one-and-a-half feet), that made the dimensions to be 150 feet by 75 feet. Inside the tent was another rectangle that God wanted constructed, and for the first time in history, the terms "the holy place," "the veil that separates," and "the Holy of Holies" became part of the nation's vernacular. No one previously, such as Abraham or Joseph, would have understood what you meant if you could have asked them about the Holy of Holies. The dimensions given for the Holy of Holies shows that it was a perfect cube being 15 feet by 15 feet by 15 feet.

The good news was that God filled His Tabernacle with His Glory; the bad news was that even Moses was not allowed to enter into it because of God's glory (Ex. 40:34-35). The good news was that God was present; the bad news was that there was a separation from Him so that only the High Priest could enter into His presence once a year with the strict dictates of the Day of Atonement (Lev. 16).

Centuries later on the exact place God had chosen—on Mount Moriah—Solomon began building God's Temple (2 Chron. 3:1-2). And in keeping with the pattern given him, Solomon made the Holy of Holies "twenty cubits in length, twenty cubits in width, and twenty cubits in height" (1 Kings 6:20), or as had been previously similar to the Tabernacle, the Holy of Holies was again a cube 30 feet by 30 feet by 30 feet. Stated differently, the Holy of Holies in God's Temple had the same dimensions as those in God's Tabernacle, only expanded. As with the Tabernacle in Exodus 40, once God's Temple was constructed, He filled it with His own glory; therefore, the priests could not enter because God's glory filled the temple (2 Chron. 7:1–2). Those who want to read more about God later removing His glory, His Temple being destroyed and then rebuilt without His Glory filling it can do so in *The Stone and the Glory*.

We know that the Temple will be rebuilt in the Tribulation. The outer court will be trampled underfoot by the Gentiles for three-and-one-half years (Rev. 11:1–2); the inner sanctum will be desecrated by the Antichrist (Matt. 24:15; 2 Thess. 2:3–4). God's Word tells us that there is currently a temple in heaven where eventually the last plagues of the Tribulation will be poured out in God's wrath (Rev. 15:5–7). Interestingly, during this time, even the holy totally sinless angels of God will not be permitted to enter into His temple because of the Glory of God (Rev. 15:8).

We have already seen aspects of New Jerusalem and matters related to God the Father, to the Lamb and to God's glory (Rev. 21:1–11). Revelation 21:10–11 gives this description:

> And he carried me away in the Spirit to a great and high mountain, and showed me the holy city, Jerusalem, coming down out of heaven from God, having the glory of God. Her brilliance was like a very costly stone, as a stone of crystal-clear jasper.

However, Revelation 21:12–13 adds this:

> It had a great and high wall, with twelve gates, and at the gates twelve angels; and names were written on them, which are those of the twelve tribes of the sons of Israel. There were three gates on the east and three gates on the north and three gates on the south and three gates on the west.

What an incredible grace given by the Godhead to the redeemed who, instead of having the one restricted entrance of both the Tabernacle and the Temple of God, will have twelve gates with twelve attending angels standing at each one in New Jerusalem. Three gates will be on each side of the compass so that wherever we will be in God's creations, we will always have a gate facing us when we look at New Jerusalem, which will most likely be visible to us no matter where we go. And the gates will always be open because it is our eternal home, because all evil will have forever been properly dealt with in final judgments of Revelation 20. Unlike the angels whom God stationed to guard access to the Tree of Life in Genesis 3, these attending angels at the twelve gates will greet and rejoice with the redeemed as they freely move and have access to all that is in heaven that the Godhead has prepared for those He loves.

Still, it is easy to overlook the importance of one verse in Revelation: "And the city is laid out as a square, and its length is as great as the width; and he measured the city with the rod, fifteen hundred miles; its length and width and height are equal" (Rev. 21:16). The New Jerusalem will have the same proportions as the Holy of Holies, only multiplied many, many times over with no restrictions or limited access. He brings His wife—the wife of the Lamb—whom He likewise calls His Bride, to His new city, as shown in Revelation 19:7–9:

> "Let us rejoice and be glad and give the glory to Him, for the marriage of the Lamb has come and His bride has

made herself ready." And it was given to her to clothe herself in fine linen, bright and clean; for the fine linen is the righteous acts of the saints. And he said to me, "Write, 'Blessed are those who are invited to the marriage supper of the Lamb.'" And he said to me, "These are true words of God."

Revelation 21:9–11 adds these details:

And one of the seven angels who had the seven bowls full of the seven last plagues, came and spoke with me, saying, "Come here, I shall show you the bride, the wife of the Lamb." And he carried me away in the Spirit to a great and high mountain, and showed me the holy city, Jerusalem, coming down out of heaven from God, having the glory of God. Her brilliance was like a very costly stone, as a stone of crystal-clear jasper.

God in His Word revealed this beautiful description of the holy city where He brings the Bride of Christ—which eventually will encompass all of the Redeemed of all time regardless of when they have or will be saved—into their holy inner sanctum so lovingly prepared by the Godhead.

We do not know exactly what we will do when we get there. We do know that in the New Jerusalem there will be no more curse, no more sin, no more temptations, no more tears, no more sorrow, no more death, no more night. And we shall dwell in the Light of His Glory (Rev. 21:23-24a) and behold Him face to face (Rev. 22:4) for all eternity—*and* that is just the beginning and a very small sampling of what God allows us to know for the time being. Oh, what treasures await throughout eternity for those who love the Lord!

Come soon, Lord Jesus!

Let not your heart be troubled; believe in God, believe also in Me. In My Father's house are many dwelling places; if it were not so, I would have told you; for I go to prepare a place for you.

And if I go and prepare a place for you, I will come again, and receive you to Myself;

that where I am, there you may be also.

—John 14:1–3

For now we see in a mirror dimly, but then face to face; now I know in part, but then I shall know fully just as I also have been fully know.

—1 Corinthians 13:12

By faith Abraham, when he was called, obeyed by going out to a place which he was to receive for an inheritance; and he went out, not knowing where he was going. By faith he lived as an alien in the land of promise, as in a foreign land, dwelling in tents with Isaac and Jacob, fellow heirs of the same promise;

for he was looking for the city which has foundations,

whose architect and builder is God.

—Hebrews 11:8–10

All these died in faith, without receiving the promises, but having seen them and having welcomed them from a distance, and having confessed that they were strangers and exiles on the earth. For those who say such things make it clear that they are seeking a country of their own. And indeed if they had been thinking of that country from which they went out, they would have had opportunity to return. But as it is, they desire a better country, that is a heavenly one. Therefore God is not ashamed to be called their God;

for He has prepared a city for them.

—Hebrews 11:13–16

See how great a love the Father has bestowed upon us, that we should be called children of God; and such we are. For this reason the world does not know us, because it did not know Him. Beloved, now we are children of God, and it has not appeared as yet what we shall be. We know that, when He appears, we shall be like Him,

> *because we shall see Him just as He is.*

And everyone who has this hope fixed on Him purifies himself, just as He is pure.

—1 John 3:1–3

And even if our gospel is veiled, it is veiled to those who are perishing, in whose case the god of this world has blinded the minds of the unbelieving,

> *that they might not see the light of the gospel of the glory of Christ,*
>
> *who is the image of God.*

For we do not preach ourselves but Christ Jesus as Lord, and ourselves as your bond-servants for Jesus' sake. For God, who said, "Light shall shine out of darkness,"

> *is the One who has shone in our hearts*
>
> *to give the light of the knowledge of the glory of God*
>
> *in the face of Christ.*

—2 Corinthians 4:3–6

"Because you have kept the word of My perseverance, I also will keep you from the hour of testing, that hour which is about to come upon the whole world, to test those who dwell upon the earth.

THE GLORY

"I am coming quickly; hold fast what you have, in order that no one take your crown. He who overcomes, I will make him a pillar in the temple of My God, and he will not go out from it anymore;

> *and I will write upon him the name of My God,*
>
> *and the name of the city of My God,*
>
> *the new Jerusalem, which comes down out of heaven from My God,*
>
> *and My new name."*
>
> —*Revelation 3:10–12*

I saw no temple in it, for the Lord God, the Almighty, and the Lamb, are its temple. And the city has no need of the sun or of the moon to shine upon it,

> *for the glory of God has illumined it,*
>
> *and its lamp is the Lamb.*
>
> —*Revelation 21:22–23*

And he showed me a river of the water of life, clear as crystal, coming from the throne of God and of the Lamb, in the middle of its street. And on either side of the river was the tree of life, bearing twelve kinds of fruit, yielding its fruit every month; and the leaves of the tree were for the healing of the nations.

And there shall no longer be any curse; and the throne of God and of the Lamb shall be in it, and His bond-servants shall serve Him;

> *and they shall see His face,*
>
> *and His name shall be on their foreheads.*
>
> —*Revelation 22:1–4*

www.ingramcontent.com/pod-product-compliance
Lightning Source LLC
Chambersburg PA
CBHW060519100426
42743CB00009B/1381